CW01454951

COMPANY MEETINGS

24th edition

COMPANY MEETINGS

24th edition

David Impey
Solicitor, Director, Jordans Professional Services Division
with

Stephen Davies
Barrister, Guildhall Chambers, Bristol

JORDANS
1999

Published by
Jordan Publishing Limited
21 St Thomas Street
Bristol BS1 6JS

British Library Cataloguing-in-Publication Data
A catalogue record for this book is available from the British Library.

ISBN 0 85308 526 9

Typeset by Mendip Communications Ltd, Frome, Somerset
Printed by MPG Books Ltd, Bodmin, Cornwall

PREFACE

The twenty-fourth edition of this book, which has appeared in previous editions under the title of *The Conduct of Meetings*, has been thoroughly revised to concentrate solely on company and insolvency meetings. The text has been updated to reflect current best practice as well as the latest important case-law and a comprehensive set of precedents has now been included.

In addition, given that such meetings may increasingly involve coordinating the efforts of people in several different countries and time zones, a new chapter has been added dealing with best practice for holding meetings by means of modern communications techniques, such as by telephone, videoconferencing or e-mail.

I would like to take this opportunity to thank Stephen Davies of Guildhall Chambers in Bristol for revising the insolvency meetings chapter and also Joanna Kennedy of Collyer-Bristow for updating the chapter dealing with speeches and defamation.

The law is stated as at 1 February 1999.

DAVID IMPEY
Bristol
February 1999

CONTENTS

TABLE OF CASES

TABLE OF STATUTES

TABLE OF STATUTORY INSTRUMENTS

Chapter 1

INTRODUCTION

THE COMPANIES ACT 1985

The meetings dealt with in this book are meetings of directors, members and creditors of companies incorporated under the Companies Act 1985 as amended ('the Act'). Many provisions regulating meetings – particularly members meetings – are to be found in the Act. References to sections are to sections in that Act unless stated otherwise.

The rules in the Act and also the rules discussed in this book apply to both companies limited by shares and companies limited by guarantee unless specified otherwise. The term 'member' is used wherever possible in this book, rather than 'shareholder', since it encompasses both members of a guarantee company and shareholders in a share company.

ARTICLES OF ASSOCIATION

Meetings are also regulated by the provisions in companies' articles of association. References to Table A are to the Table A in the Companies (Tables A to F) Regulations 1985, SI 1985/805 as amended by SI 1985/1052. By virtue of s 8(2) the regulations in Table A constitute the articles of association of a company limited by shares as if articles in the form of Table A had been registered by the company at Companies House. A company limited by shares which does not register any articles of its own at Companies House will find that the regulations in Table A apply in their entirety as its articles of association. Alternatively a company limited by shares may register its own articles which exclude or modify the application of Table A. This is almost invariably what happens. A listed public company will, for example, exclude Table A entirely and register its own articles of association at Companies House since this is required by the Stock Exchange. The articles of a small private company limited by shares are more likely to provide that 'Table A shall apply save as follows'. The remainder of the articles will comprise a series of exclusions of, or modifications to, particular regulations in Table A.

The 1985 Table A is merely the latest in a series of Tables A. If a particular Table A applied to a company when it was incorporated, that Table A continues to apply notwithstanding the subsequent introduction of new versions of Table A into the general law. It is only if the company adopts an entirely new set of articles that the version of Table A which is in force at the date of adoption will supersede the original Table A in its application to that company. Mere amendments to the original articles by the company will not have the same effect. The original version of Table A will continue to apply. As a general principle a company limited by shares should consider whether it needs to adopt a new set of articles at least every time a new version of Table A is introduced and whenever the Companies Act is amended.

Even in the case of two companies both of whose articles cross-refer to the same Table A, there may be significant differences between the rules which apply in relation to meetings in each case. Very different variations may have been made to that Table A by each company. The need to consult and consider the articles of each individual company cannot be overstated. It must not be assumed that there are 'usual' provisions which apply. A person concerned with meetings of a share company is therefore likely to need to keep a copy of the company's articles and the right version of Table A to hand at all times.

The differences in companies' articles are hardly surprising given the many different types of company. The operation of a small private company, a large public company with thousands of shareholders, and a not for profit company limited by guarantee will inevitably be quite different and this will be reflected in their constitutions.

A company limited by guarantee must register its own articles of association at Companies House. If it fails to do so, Table A will not apply in default as it would in the case of a company limited by shares. Instead the company will have no articles. The form of the articles of a company limited by guarantee are required, by s 8(4), to follow Table C in the Companies (Tables A to F) Regulations 1985, SI 1985/805 as amended 'or as near to that form as circumstances admit'.

Confusingly, Table C itself cross-refers to Table A, but excludes and modifies the provisions of Table A which refer to share capital. Such provisions are, of course, inappropriate to a company limited by guarantee. Those concerned with meetings of guarantee companies will therefore need to equip themselves with a copy of their own articles of association, Table C and also Table A.

Most guarantee companies take advantage of the 'as near to that form as circumstances admit' concession. The variations likely to be found between, for example, the rules relating to meetings which appear in the constitution of a charitable company limited by guarantee and those which appear in a residents' property management company or incorporated sports club, both of which are also likely to be companies limited by guarantee, are significant. This book does not address the particular requirements of such companies. See instead, *Running a Charity* and *Running a Flat Management Company*.[1] The warning that each company's articles must be consulted and carefully considered to determine the specific rules applicable to the particular company must be sounded even more loudly in relation to guarantee companies than share companies.

INFORMAL RULES

The company may also operate according to informal rules which supplement the requirements of the Act and articles of association. These may be set out in, for example, operating manuals or like documents, decided upon from time to time by the directors.

CUSTOM

There may also be customs followed by the company generally, or at a number of previous meetings, which have acquired some status by virtue of the fact that members or directors have an expectation that they will be followed.

GENERAL PRINCIPLES

Finally, in the absence of regulation by the Act, the articles, any informal rules or custom, there is a body of general principles which may apply to company meetings by virtue of the common law, as established by the courts over the centuries.

These various rules operate as a hierarchy. Customs may not be inconsistent with operating procedures; operating procedures may not be inconsistent with articles of association and so on. The common law provides the final layer of guidance in the event that the solution to a problem cannot be found at a higher level in the hierarchy.

CADBURY, GREENBURY AND HAMPEL

For listed and AIM[2] companies, there are additional layers of regulation contained in the rules of the Stock Exchange and AIM. In addition, concerns over corporate

---

1   Francesca Quint *Running a Charity* 2nd edn (Jordans, 1997); Nigel G Cox *Running a Flat Management Company* 2nd edn (Jordans, 1993).
2   Alternative Investment Market.

governance and directors' remuneration have led to the establishment of a number of committees to review corporate practices and consequent publication of Reports and Codes of Practice. These are the Cadbury Report,[3] including the Cadbury Code of Best Practice, the Greenbury Report[4] and the Hampel Report.[5] Whilst they are not statutory, adherence to the recommendations in these Reports is encouraged through monitoring of such companies' compliance by the Stock Exchange and AIM.

Some of the recommendations of the different Committees do relate to meetings of directors and members, but these will already be familiar to officers of companies affected by them. For this reason, and because corporate governance is so fast-moving, they have not been addressed specifically in this book

However, those recommendations also provide examples of best practice to which other large companies may usefully aspire. For example, larger non-listed companies might consider the Hampel recommendations that companies whose annual general meetings are well attended could include a presentation followed by a question and answer session at the meeting, and that the chairman should provide a subsequent written answer to any important questions raised but not answered at the meeting. Other innovative proposals, designed to achieve parity between private and institutional investors, include a requirement to despatch to shareholders a précis of proceedings to shareholders who request one, and regional seminars and briefings for brokers acting for private clients.

Consequently, readers wishing to learn more are recommended to obtain copies of the Reports and also the excellent guides on the interpretation and application of many of the recommendations produced by bodies such as the City Group for Smaller Companies ('CISCO') and the Institute of Chartered Secretaries and Administrators ('ICSA').[6]

---

3   'The Financial Aspects of Corporate Governance'. The Report was published in 1992 and included a 'Code of Best Practice'. This has now been incorporated in large parts into the Combined Code, which consolidates the provisions arising from Cadbury, Greenbury and Hampel.
4   'Report on Directors' Remuneration' published July 1995.
5   'The Hampel Report' of the Hampel Committee on Corporate Governance published January 1998.
6   CISCO's 'Guidance for Smaller Companies On the Cadbury Code' and ICSA's 'Guide to Best Practice for Annual General Meetings'.

Chapter 2

THE CONTROL AND MANAGEMENT OF COMPANIES

DIVISION OF POWERS

A company is recognised in law as being a distinct legal person.[1] However, being an artificial entity, it is only capable of acting through its duly constituted organs. These organs are the members entitled to vote, acting in general meeting, and the board of directors. The Companies Act 1985 provides that certain decisions may only be made by one or other organ of the company. So far as the members acting in general meeting are concerned, the Act lays down four particular ways in which the members may make a decision or 'resolution'. These are by special resolution, extraordinary resolution, ordinary resolution and elective resolution. Special resolutions and extraordinary resolutions require, in order to be passed, a three-fourths majority of the votes cast at the meeting. An ordinary resolution requires a simple majority. Elective resolutions require unanimous agreement by all members entitled to attend and vote.

The members may also make decisions without holding a general meeting. Instead, every member entitled to attend and vote can sign a written resolution in lieu of holding a general meeting. A written resolution can comprise several documents in like form, each signed by one or more members, but the overriding requirement is that all members entitled to attend and vote must sign.[2]

Those powers which are not required by the Act to be exercised by a particular organ are normally divided between the corporate organs by the company's articles of association. The provisions of the articles of association cannot, however, have the effect of relaxing the provisions of the Act. This means that where the Act requires certain decisions to be made in general meeting by special or extraordinary resolution, the articles may not provide for them to be made by a lesser majority. On the other hand, anything which may be done by a simple majority can, under the articles of association, be required to be done by a greater majority.

---

1   *Salomon v Salomon & Co* [1897] AC 22, HL.
2   Such written resolutions may be valid as 'informal corporate acts' or, in the case of a private company, because they are passed as statutory written resolutions pursuant to the Act. See Chapter 3.

The articles of association are one of the two constituent documents of the company. (The other is the memorandum of association.) The articles lay down the rules by which the company will conduct its affairs. They may only be altered by special resolution,[3] and then only within the parameters laid down by the mandatory provisions of the Act. As discussed in Chapter 1, a company limited by shares, which is the most common form of company, usually adopts Table A with some amendments. If the articles do not address a particular matter dealt with in Table A, the relevant provisions of Table A will apply. If the same company lodges no articles of association of its own at the time of its registration then Table A will become that company's articles in its entirety.[4]

Unless the Act or the articles otherwise provide, a company can authorise any decision by an ordinary resolution, that is, one passed at a general meeting by a bare majority of votes.

> 'Unless some provision to the contrary is to be found in the charter or other instrument by which the company is incorporated, the resolution of a majority of the shareholders, duly convened, upon any question with which the company is legally competent to deal, is binding upon the minority, and consequently upon the company, and every shareholder has a perfect right to vote upon any such question, although he may have a personal interest in the subject-matter opposed to, or different from, the general or particular interests of the company.'[5]

This is, however, limited to matters which the company is legally entitled to transact. If all the members agree to a corporate act which is illegal or unlawful, this is ineffective and the company does not thereby acquire the power necessary for that purpose. It is also the case that if the articles or the Act have removed control of certain matters from the general meeting, then the majority of members will not have any power in relation to those matters. Where the articles (rather than the Act) have deprived the general meeting of power, however, it is always open to the company to alter the articles by special resolution.

Most company articles provide that the business of the company shall be managed by the directors. Where the articles provide to this effect, then the power of the members in general meeting to interfere with the running of the company is very limited. Nevertheless, there are circumstances where, notwithstanding the fact that the power to manage the business of the company resides with the directors, the general meeting may exercise the management power. This power will transfer to the general meeting if the directors waive their power, are unable to exercise it because of conflicting personal interests, are deadlocked or are inquorate. In these circumstances, the general meeting may act by ordinary resolution.[6]

---

3   Companies Act 1985, s 9.
4   Ibid, s 8(2).
5   *North-West Transportation Co v Beatty* (1887) 12 App Cas 589, 593. But for a very different approach to personal interests, see *Clemens v Clemens Bros Ltd* [1976] 2 All ER 268.
6   *Barron v Potter* [1914] 1 Ch 895; *Foster v Foster* [1916] 1 Ch 532.

The provision of Table A which confers on the directors the power to manage the company's business is reg 70. This regulation provides as follows:

> 'Subject to the provisions of the Act, the memorandum and the articles and to any directions given by special resolution, the business of the company shall be managed by the directors who may exercise all the powers of the company. No alteration of the memorandum or articles and no such direction shall invalidate any prior act of the directors which would have been valid if that alteration had not been made or that direction had not been given. The powers given by this regulation shall not be limited to any special power given to the directors by the articles and a meeting of directors at which a quorum is present may exercise all powers exercisable by the directors.'

If the members of a company disapprove of the action of its directors on a matter which is within the powers of the directors, they cannot, by passing a resolution, annul the directors' decision. The members can remove the directors by ordinary resolution (see Chapter 3) or, by special resolution, control the directors for the future by altering the articles. Where the company has an article in the form of reg 70, then the general meeting may also control the directors for the future by giving directions by special resolution; however, such directions cannot invalidate an act which has already been carried out by the directors.

ULTRA VIRES ACTS

If a company acts outside the powers conferred on it by its memorandum of association, this does not render the relevant act invalid.[7] However, a member may bring proceedings to restrain an act outside the powers conferred on the company in the memorandum, although these proceedings cannot be brought where the act to be done is 'in fulfilment of a legal obligation arising from a previous act of the company'.[8] It should, however, be noted that the directors are liable for breach of duty if they are responsible for the company acting outside the powers laid down in its memorandum. They may only escape liability for this breach of duty if the general meeting passes a special resolution specifically relieving them from their breach. A special resolution which merely ratifies the decision is insufficient to save the directors from the consequences of their breach of duty.[9]

Where the directors act outside the range of powers allocated to them by the Act and the articles of association by, for example, usurping powers which belong to the general meeting, then the act of the directors will still be valid in favour of a person dealing with the company in good faith.[10] Members have the right to bring proceedings to restrain the doing of an act which is beyond the power of the

---

7 Companies Act 1985, s 35(1).
8 Ibid, s 35(2).
9 Ibid, s 35(3).
10 Ibid, s 35A(1).

directors, but this right is subject to the same limitations, as discussed above, as the right to restrain the doing of an act which is outside the capacity of the company as laid down in its memorandum.[11]

Where the directors act outside the powers allocated to them then they are liable for a breach of duty to the company.[12] It seems likely that an ordinary resolution of the company is sufficient to excuse the directors from this breach of duty, although directors wishing to ensure their position beyond doubt in such circumstances would be advised to seek the passing of a special resolution excusing them from liability.

COMMENCEMENT OF LITIGATION

It seems that where companies have an article in the form of reg 70 then the power to initiate litigation belongs to the board of directors.[13] The case of *John Shaw & Sons (Salford) Ltd v Shaw*[14] makes it clear that, where the board of directors has been delegated general powers of management, the general meeting is incapable of discontinuing litigation initiated by the board. Possibly, however, where the company has an article in the form of reg 70, the general meeting may be able to direct the board of directors by special resolution to discontinue litigation. Where the directors' decision not to commence litigation is in breach of their duties to the company then it seems that the general meeting has the right to initiate the relevant litigation.[15] It is also the case that the general meeting has the right to commence proceedings in the name of the company against the directors for breach of their duty.[16]

The circumstances in which a minority of members can bring an action in the name of the company are very limited. They may do so, using the form of action known as the derivative action, where there is a fraud on the minority.[17] A minority member is not, however, permitted to bring an action in its own name for a wrong done to the company. This would breach the rule in *Foss v Harbottle*, which stipulates that the proper plaintiff for a wrong done to the company is the company

---

11   Companies Act 1985, s 35A(4).
12   Ibid, s 35A(5).
13   Compare the approaches in *Marshall's Valve Gear Co Ltd v Manning, Wardle & Co Ltd* [1909] 1 Ch 267 and *John Shaw & Sons (Salford) Ltd v Shaw* [1935] 2 KB 113, HL.
14   [1935] 2 KB 113, HL.
15   *Re Argentum* [1975] 1 All ER 608, which explains *Marshall's Valve Gear Co Ltd v Manning, Wardle & Co Ltd, supra,* on this basis.
16   *Pender v Lushington* (1877) 6 ChD 70.
17   See, for example, *Burland v Earle* [1902] AC 83; *Menier v Hooper's Telegraph Co* (1874) LR 9 Ch App 350; *Pavlides v Jensen* [1956] Ch 565; *Prudential Assurance Co Ltd v Newman Industries Ltd (No 2)* [1982] 2 WLR 31.

itself.[18] Any member, all the members or some part of the membership, including the petitioning member may, nevertheless, petition the court under s 459 of the Act on the basis that the affairs of the company are being conducted in a manner which is unfairly prejudicial to company members. They may also petition for the winding up of the company on 'just and equitable' grounds.[19]

At the time of writing the Law Commission has published recommendations[20] that the law relating to shareholder remedies should be revised to make it simpler and more accessible. Particularly, the rule in *Foss v Harbottle* is singled out for abolition. However, substantive changes to the law are unlikely until the Department of Trade and Industry have consulted more fully on their proposals for a root and branch reform of company law generally.

---

18   (1843) 2 Hare 461.
19   Insolvency Act 1986, s 122(1)(g).
20   Cm 246 (1997).

Chapter 3

TYPES OF MEMBERS' RESOLUTION

INTRODUCTION

There are four types of resolution which may be put to a members' meeting: ordinary, extraordinary, special and elective. It should be noted, however, that companies may also pass resolutions without a meeting. This may occur where a company passes a resolution by an informal corporate act or where a private company passes a resolution under the statutory written resolution procedure introduced by the Companies Act 1989.

ORDINARY RESOLUTIONS

Ordinary resolutions are usually referred to in the Act as resolutions of the company in general meeting, and are those which are passed by a bare majority of those voting at any kind of general meeting.

As has been pointed out, the articles may allocate certain powers to the board of directors in such a way that those powers can no longer be exercised by the company in general meeting. Apart from decisions which have been thus assigned to the board, a company may make by ordinary resolution all such decisions as are not required by the Act or by its articles to be effected by special or extraordinary resolution. There are, however, a number of decisions which a company is expressly empowered by the Act to decide by resolution of the company in general meeting, that is, by an ordinary resolution. For example, s 121 provides in certain cases that the company in general meeting may, if so authorised by its articles, make certain changes to the conditions in its memorandum. Changes in capital structure, for example, (not including reduction) are permitted under this section. The fact that the Act gives such power does not mean that the articles may not require something more stringent, and the articles of private companies frequently provide that changes in capital require a special resolution.

The one case in the Act where there is specific reference to an ordinary resolution is s 303, which provides that a company may by ordinary resolution remove a director before the expiration of the director's period of office, notwithstanding anything in its articles or in any agreement between the company and the director.

Special notice is required of any resolution to remove a director under this section or to appoint at the same meeting a director to replace the director so removed. The meaning of special notice is considered below.

On receipt of notice of an intended resolution to remove a director under s 303 the company is bound forthwith to send a copy of the notice to the director concerned, and the director (whether or not a member of the company) is entitled to be heard on the resolution at the meeting (s 304(1)). The company is also obliged to circulate representations in writing by the director or to allow such representations to be read out at the meeting (s 304(2) and (3)). This provision on directors' representations is subject, however, to the court being satisfied, on the application of the company or any other aggrieved person, that the circulation of the director's representation is not being used in order to secure needless publicity for defamatory material (s 304(4)).

Although s 303 requires that special notice be given of a resolution to remove a director under the section, it does not require that the resolution be proposed by the person who gave the special notice. Once someone has given special notice, that person or any other member entitled to vote may propose the resolution. It is to be noted that the Act does not itself authorise the appointment of some other person in place of a director removed in this way; this is left to the articles. All that is provided in this respect is special notice of any intention to appoint someone else, and that if a vacancy caused by a removal is not filled at the meeting it may be filled as a casual vacancy (s 303(3)), which again leads back to the articles to discover who has the power to fill the vacancy and how. Where the vacancy is filled at the same meeting at which the director is removed then the person so appointed is, for the purpose of ascertaining which directors are to retire by rotation, deemed to have been appointed on the day the removed director was last appointed a director (s 303(4)). So far as the director who has been removed at the meeting is concerned, the section does not deprive that director of compensation or damages payable in respect of the termination of his or her appointment as director or of any other appointment terminating with the appointment as director, for example as managing director, and is not to interfere with any other power that the company may have of removing a director (s 303(5)).

The provisions of s 303 override anything to the contrary in the articles. Subsection (5) makes it clear, however, that the procedure for removing a director in s 303 is not the only procedure which may be used by the company. It seems that the power in s 303 is additional to any other powers which the company may have to remove a director. If members consider that ss 303 and 304 offer too much protection to directors, they may include a simpler procedure for removing directors in the company's articles. Thus, provisions in company articles which provide for removal of a director by, for example, extraordinary resolution, may be used by the company without the need for compliance with any of the requirements of ss 303 and 304, including the requirement of special notice. Likewise, it seems to be the case that if the articles provide for removal by service of a notice of removal signed by a majority shareholder on the registered office of the company, such a provision may also be relied upon to the exclusion of the requirements in ss 303 and 304.

Conversely in some companies the provisions of s 303 may be considered insufficient protection for directors. In such cases, special articles are often incorporated which give special rights to the directors if an attempt is made to remove them from office. The classic example of this occurred in *Bushell v Faith*,[1] in which the House of Lords upheld the validity of an article giving extra votes to a director on a resolution to remove him.[2] The director also held shares in the company and was entitled to vote on the resolution for his own removal. Naturally, he voted against the resolution, which was not passed. Despite what Lord Morris said in that case by way of dissent, such articles are sometimes important or even essential in order to safeguard the interests of persons who may, for example, have incorporated a company to be operated as a quasi-partnership. On the other hand, larger companies would have little legitimate use for such a provision, and no listed company could have such an article.

SPECIAL NOTICE

Special notice of an ordinary resolution is required by the Act in three classes of cases. One of these relates to the removal of a director under s 303, the provisions of which are discussed immediately above. The other circumstances in which the Act requires special notice for a resolution relate to the position of the auditor and the appointment of a director over the age of 70. In relation to auditors, special notice is required for: a resolution to fill a casual vacancy in the office of the auditor (s 388(3)(a)); a resolution to reappoint a retiring auditor who was appointed by the directors to fill a casual vacancy (s 388(3)(b)); a resolution to remove an auditor before the expiration of the auditor's term of office (s 391A(1)(a)); and a resolution appointing as auditor a person other than a retiring auditor (s 391A(1)(b)). So far as the appointment of a director over the age of 70 is concerned, s 293(5) provides that special notice must be given of a resolution appointing such a person as a director of a public company or a private company which is a subsidiary of a public company (including a Northern Ireland public company).

The special notice required in the case of resolutions of the three cases just mentioned is dealt with by s 379, which provides that, where special notice is required of a resolution, the resolution shall not be effective unless notice of the intention to move it has been given to the company not less than 28 days before the meeting at which it is moved. It also provides that the company shall give its members notice of any such resolution at the same time and in the same manner as

---

1   [1970] AC 1099.
2   See Appendix for such an article.

it gives notice of the meeting or, if that is not practicable, shall give them notice, either by advertisement in a newspaper having an appropriate circulation or in any other way allowed by the articles, not less than 21 days before the meeting.

A proviso (s 379(3)) lays down that if, after notice has been given to the company, a meeting is called for a date 28 days or less after the notice has been given, the notice though not given within the time required by the section shall be deemed to have been properly given for the purposes thereof. This achieves the dual purpose of ensuring first, that the directors cannot frustrate the proposal by promptly calling a meeting without the removal resolution, and, secondly, of making effective a resolution for removing a director even if, for convenience or to save expense or by necessity, the meeting is called for holding within the specified 28 days.

It will be noted that the requirements as to special notice are twofold. First, notice of the intention to move the resolution must be given to the company not less than 28 days before the meeting at which it is to be moved, and consequently even if the board desire to put forward a resolution for which special notice is required, they must arrange for someone to give this notice to the company. This notice should be given by a person who, being entitled to do so, intends to propose the resolution, but provided that such notice has been duly given, any member may in fact propose the resolution. Secondly, on receipt of this notice the board 'shall' give notice of the proposed resolution to the members in the same way as it gives notice to the meeting. This does not, however, confer on an individual member any right to compel the board to include the resolution in the agenda for a meeting, and is merely part of the machinery to ensure that members will have, subject to the proviso, at least 21 days' notice of a resolution requiring the special notice procedure.[3] The member who gives special notice to the company can insist on the resolution going into the agenda only if there is a provision to this effect in the articles or if the member can invoke s 376 (which is discussed in Chapter 5).

Nor does receipt by the company of notice of an intention to move a resolution under this section compel the company to hold a meeting. If the notice signifies the intention to move the resolution at the next meeting the board need not give notice of it until the next annual general meeting is held, unless an extraordinary general meeting is either convened in the ordinary way or requisitioned under s 368 before the date for the annual general meeting. If, therefore, the next meeting is not an annual general meeting, it will be sufficient to give 14 days' notice of the resolution (s 379(3)). If, however, it is impracticable for notice of the intended resolution to be given in the same way as notice of the meeting is given, then in any case, subject, again, to the proviso in s 379(3), 21 days' notice thereof must be given either by advertisement in a newspaper or in any other way allowed by the articles.

The provisions in s 381A on written resolutions of private companies do not apply to resolutions removing a director under s 303 or removing an auditor before the

---

3   *Pedley v Inland Waterways Association Ltd* [1977] 1 All ER 209.

expiration of the term of the auditor's office under s 391 (s 381A(7)). It is clear that a statutory written resolution will be ineffective where special notice is required. However, this does still leave some scope for confusion about the application of the special notice provisions to the law on informal corporate acts. Further attention is given to these matters below.

EXTRAORDINARY RESOLUTIONS

The Companies Act 1985 and the Insolvency Act 1986 (IA 1986) provide that certain actions may be taken only by extraordinary resolution. This is a right of the members, and cannot be excluded by the articles. Those actions which may only be carried out by extraordinary resolution are: resolving that a company shall be wound up on the grounds that it cannot by reason of its liabilities continue its business (IA 1986, s 84(1)(c)); sanctioning the exercise by the liquidator of certain powers in a members' voluntary winding up (IA 1986, s 165(2)(a)); and certain variations of class rights (s 125(2)). In addition, articles sometimes provide that certain actions, for example the removal of a director without going through the formalities of giving special notice, may be effected by extraordinary resolution.

Section 378(1) provides that an extraordinary resolution is one which has been passed by not less than three-fourths of such members, as being entitled to do so, vote in person or, where proxies are allowed, by proxy at a general meeting of which notice specifying the intention to propose the resolution as an extraordinary resolution has been duly given. This subsection deals only with voting on a show of hands. Unless the articles otherwise provide, which they very seldom do, only members personally present are counted on a show of hands, not those present by proxy. The position on a poll is dealt with by s 378(5), which provides that in computing the majority on a poll demanded on the question that an extraordinary resolution or a special resolution be passed, reference shall be had to the number of votes cast for and against the resolution. In summary, for a special or extraordinary resolution to be passed on a show of hands at least 75 per cent of the members voting must vote in its favour, and on a poll 75 per cent of the total votes validly cast (which will include votes cast by proxies) must be in favour of the resolution.

The notice of the meeting at which it is intended to propose a resolution as an extraordinary resolution must set out the exact words of the resolution or its entire substance, and also that it is intended to propose the resolution as an extraordinary resolution.[4] As noted in Chapter 5, under s 369 the length of notice of a meeting (other than the annual general meeting) for passing an extraordinary resolution by a company other than an unlimited company is 14 clear days, unless a shorter notice is agreed to in the manner specified in s 369(3).

---

4   *McConnell v Prill & Co* [1916] 2 Ch 57.

The relationship between the requirements for an extraordinary resolution and a resolution passed by an informal corporate act was considered in *Re Oxted Motor Company*.[5] In this case, it was held that an extraordinary resolution for voluntary winding up might be passed by the unanimous consent of all the members, even though no notice had been given. This is, of course, consistent with the general principle underlying the doctrine of informal corporate acts that all the members can consent to any proposal within the company's powers unless the Act imposes any outside restriction, such as the consent of the court. It should also be noted that, quite apart from the doctrine of informal corporate acts, it is possible for voting members holding 95 per cent in nominal value of the shares or, where there is no share capital, representing 95 per cent of the voting rights, to agree to short notice for an extraordinary resolution (s 369(3) and (4)).

SPECIAL RESOLUTIONS

Special resolutions are required by the Act or the Insolvency Act for various purposes, of which some of the more significant are:

(1) altering the articles (s 9);
(2) altering the objects clause in the memorandum or conditions in the memorandum which could have been in the articles of association (ss 4 and 17);
(3) changing the company's name (s 28);
(4) disapplying members' statutory pre-emption rights (s 95);
(5) approving, where permissible, the provision of financial assistance for the purpose of shares or agreements for the purchase of its own shares by a private company (s 155 and s 164);
(6) reducing capital (s 135);
(7) procuring the winding up of the company by the court (IA 1986, s 122(1)); and
(8) voluntarily winding up the company (IA 1986, s 84(1)(b)).

In addition, the articles may provide that the company is only able to do certain things by special (or extraordinary) resolution.

Section 378(2) lays down the requirements for the passing of a special resolution. These are the same as the requirements for the passing of an extraordinary resolution, except that instead of 14 days' notice, 21 days' notice is required, and the resolution must be specified in the notice as a special resolution. The majority required is the same as for an extraordinary resolution, that is three-fourths of those entitled to vote on a show of hands or three-fourths of votes cast on a poll. The

---

5   [1921] 3 KB 32.

provisions governing voting by show of hands and poll, and on short notice (see s 378(3)), are the same for extraordinary resolutions and special resolutions.

Pursuant to the doctrine of informal corporate acts, a special resolution may be passed with no notice if all members entitled to attend and vote agree to it.[6] Indeed, as discussed below, a meeting is not even necessary for the application of the doctrine of informal corporate acts.

AMENDMENTS TO PROPOSED RESOLUTIONS

(1) Special and extraordinary resolutions

Unless all the members entitled to attend and vote agree, the basic rule is that no amendment may be made to a proposed special or extraordinary resolution.[7] The only special or extraordinary resolution which may, therefore, be passed is that specified in the notice for the resolution. The rule includes circulars accompanying such notices. In *Moorgate Mercantile Holdings Ltd*,[8] a derogation from this general rule was allowed. It was held that a special or extraordinary resolution

> 'as passed can properly be regarded as "the resolution" identified in the proceeding notice even though (a) it departs in some respects from the text of a resolution set out in such notice (for example by correcting those grammatical or clerical errors which can be corrected as a matter of construction, or by reducing the words to more formal language) or (b) it is reduced into the form of a new text which was not included in the notice, provided only that in either case there is no departure whatever from the substance.'[9]

(2) Ordinary resolutions

The position is less stringent in relation to proposed ordinary resolutions. Nevertheless, any amendment to an ordinary resolution must be within the scope of the notice convening the meeting. This principle has been interpreted broadly so that in *Betts & Co v MacNaghten*[10] where notice was given of a resolution to appoint three named directors, an amendment to appoint two additional directors was held to be valid. In that case, however, notice was given of the resolution with the addition of the words 'with such amendments as shall be determined on at the meeting'. Similarly, in *Choppington Collieries v Johnson*,[11] the articles provided that the election of directors in place of those retiring by rotation was not special

---

6   *Cane v Jones* [1981] 1 All ER 533.
7   *Re Moorgate Mercantile Holdings Ltd* [1980] 1 WLR 227.
8   [1980] 1 WLR 227.
9   Ibid.
10 [1910] 1 Ch 430.
11 [1944] 1 All ER 762.

business. Notice was sent out of an annual general meeting stating that the business was, inter alia, to elect directors (in the plural) and also stating that one retiring director offered himself for re-election. It was held that the meeting could appoint persons other than the retiring director to be directors up to the maximum number allowed by the articles. This is consistent with the principle that an amendment should not impose a greater burden on the company than the original motion.

A proposed amendment to an ordinary resolution need not be in writing unless the articles expressly provide, but it should be sufficiently definite.[12] The proposed amendment must be put to the meeting, but need not be seconded unless the articles specifically require this. 'If the chairman put the question without its being proposed or seconded by anybody, that would be perfectly good'.[13] A chairman is, therefore, not justified in refusing a motion or amendment because there is no seconder unless the articles expressly provide that all motions and amendments shall be seconded. If the mover of an amendment does not challenge the chairman's ruling that an amendment should not be put, that is not a waiver of the mover's right to impeach the resolution.[14]

Where the amendments number more than one, these should be put to the meeting in the order in which they affect the main question and then the main question in its original form or as finally amended should be put to the meeting. Strict adherence to the formality of putting motions and amendments is not essential, provided they are put to the meeting in such a way that those present understand what it is that they are called upon to decide.[15]

ELECTIVE RESOLUTIONS

The Companies Act 1989 introduced an elective regime for private companies into the Act. Section 379A(1) provides that an elective resolution may be passed by a private company making an election to do any one of the following things:

(a) to remove or extend the duration of authority to allot shares (s 80A);
(b) to dispense with the laying of accounts and reports before the general meeting (s 252);
(c) to dispense with the holding of annual general meetings (s 366A);
(d) to reduce the majority required to authorise short notice of a meeting (ss 369(4) and 378(3)); and
(e) to dispense with the appointment of auditors annually (s 386).

---

12   *Henderson v Bank of Australasia* (1890) 45 ChD 330.
13   *Re Horbury Bridge Coal Co* (1879) 11 ChD 109 at 118.
14   *Henderson v Bank of Australasia* (1890) 45 ChD 330 at 350.
15   *Stevens ex parte* (1852) 16 JP 632.

An elective resolution may only be passed at a meeting of which 21 days' notice in writing is given, and for which the notice states that an elective resolution is to be proposed and also states the terms of the proposed elective resolution (s 379A(2) (a)). All members entitled to vote in person or by proxy must agree to the passing of the elective resolution (s 379A(2)(b)). Notwithstanding this stringent requirement, the elective resolution may be revoked by an ordinary resolution (s 379A(3)). It also ceases to have effect if the company becomes a public company (s 379A(4)).

The most obvious impact of this elective regime on the matters previously discussed is s 379A(1)(d) which allows an elective resolution to permit short notice for a meeting or for a special resolution to be agreed to by the holders of 90 per cent in nominal value of the shares carrying the right to attend and vote or, where the company does not have a share capital, 90 per cent of the total voting rights at the meeting, rather than 95 per cent as stipulated in s 369(4) in relation to notice for meetings and s 378(3) in relation to notice for special resolutions.

INFORMAL CORPORATE ACTS AND WRITTEN RESOLUTIONS IN LIEU OF A MEMBERS' MEETING

The common law doctrine of informal corporate acts and the statutory provisions for written resolutions in lieu of a members' meeting by private companies co-exist, slightly uneasily, with each other. Section 381C(2)(b) seems to be intended expressly to preserve the common law doctrine.

The common law doctrine of informal corporate acts applies in theory to any type of company, but in practice will probably only be used by those companies with a relatively limited membership. As indicated earlier in this work, the effect of the doctrine is that, provided the matter is intra vires the company, the agreement of all members entitled to attend and vote at a company meeting is binding on the company.[16] No meeting is necessary.[17]

There is some confusion as to whether those entitled to be heard, but not to vote, at a company meeting must also assent in order for there to be an informal corporate act. This issue was raised in *Duomatic Ltd*[18] but, on the facts of the case, it was not necessary to decide it because the non-voting shareholders in question had no actual right under the articles to attend or to be heard at the meeting. Nevertheless, the case is not generally regarded as supporting the proposition that those with the right to attend and be heard must assent in order for there to be a valid informal corporate act.

---

16 *Parker & Cooper v Reading Ltd* [1926] Ch 975.
17 Ibid.
18 [1969] 2 WLR 114.

What is clear is that an informal corporate act can achieve what may only otherwise be achieved by extraordinary[19] or special resolution,[20] without the need for any of the formalities normally associated with such resolutions. Whether an informal corporate act can cure the absence of special notice as required by s 379 is a more vexed question. On general principles, one might have assumed the answer to be in the affirmative, but some doubt arises as a result of the fact that the provisions for special notice are intended to protect the director or auditor to be removed rather than the members and the better view may, therefore, be that their unanimous consent is not to the point.

Section 381A(1) allows a private company to do anything which might be done by a resolution in general meeting or by a resolution passed at a meeting of any class of members of the company by a written resolution signed by all members entitled to attend and vote at the meeting. It is not necessary for the signatures of the members to be on a single document (s 381A(2)). As noted earlier, a resolution removing a director before the expiration of their term of office under s 303 or a resolution removing an auditor before the expiration of their term of office under s 391 cannot be passed using this statutory written resolution procedure (s 381A (7)). Subject to this, the procedure may be used to pass any resolution, including a special, extraordinary or elective resolution (s 381A(6)).

Initially some confusion existed about the relationship between s 381A and reg 53 of Table A, which allows for a resolution in writing without the exceptions and other requirements contained in ss 381A to 381C. It is now clear that an article in the form of reg 53 provides an alternative method of passing a resolution to that laid down in s 381A (rather than reg 53 being subject to the statutory regime for written resolutions in ss 381A to 381C). Whether a written resolution under reg 53 can cure the absence of special notice as required by s 379 is as vexed a question as it was in the context of informal corporate acts. Again, the better view is probably that it cannot.

The provisions for written resolutions in ss 381A to 381C are, in some respects, narrower than the doctrine of informal corporate acts as they apply only to private companies. On the other hand, it is arguable that in two respects the statutory provisions for written resolutions cover wider ground than the common law doctrine of informal corporate acts. First, it may be that the power of the company to alter its share capital under s 121 cannot be exercised by an informal corporate act. The basis of this argument is the unusually specific provision in s 121(4) which provides that 'The powers conferred by this section must be exercised by the company in general meeting'. This may pre-empt the application of the doctrine of informal corporate acts, but it is generally thought that the wording of s 381A(1) would permit a private company to pass a written resolution to alter its share

19   *Re Oxted Motor Co* [1921] 2 KB 32.
20   *Cane v Jones* [1981] 1 All ER 533.

capital. Secondly, s 381A(6) specifically includes elective resolutions within the ambit of the statutory procedure for written resolutions. It is, however, open to doubt whether an elective resolution could be effected by an informal corporate act as a written resolution pursuant to reg 53. The reason for this doubt arises from the wording of s 379A(2)(b) which provides that the resolution must be 'agreed to at the meeting'.

REGISTRATION OF RESOLUTIONS

Section 380(1) requires that certain resolutions and agreements must be lodged with the Registrar of Companies within 15 days of their passing or making. The Registrar is obliged to record the relevant resolution. The same types of resolutions and agreements which must be lodged with the Registrar must also be embodied in, or annexed to, every copy of the articles issued after the passing of the resolution or the making of the agreement (s 380(2)).

The resolutions and agreements to which these provisions apply are listed in s 380(4). They include resolutions of the type listed below which are effected by an informal corporate act, a written resolution pursuant to reg 53 in Table A or by written resolution under s 381A. The resolutions in question are as follows: special resolutions; extraordinary resolutions; elective resolutions and resolutions revoking elective resolutions; resolutions of, or binding members of, a class of shareholders; resolutions passed by company directors in order to effect a change of company name on the direction of the Secretary of State under s 31(2); resolutions to give, vary, revoke or renew an authority to the directors for the allotment of certain securities under s 80; a resolution of the directors to alter the company memorandum on the company ceasing to be a public company under s 147(2); a resolution conferring, varying, revoking or renewing authority for a market purchase by the company of its own shares under s 166; a resolution for voluntary winding up under s 84(1)(a) of the Insolvency Act; and a resolution of the directors of an old public company that the company should be re-registered as a public company under s 2(1) of the Companies Consolidation (Consequential Provisions) Act 1985.

Failure to comply with the provisions of s 380 as to lodgement with the Registrar and as to annexation to the articles makes the company and every officer in default liable to a fine (s 380(5) and (6)).

Chapter 4

MEETINGS OF MEMBERS (INCLUDING CLASSES OF MEMBERS AND OF DEBENTURE HOLDERS)

ANNUAL GENERAL MEETINGS

Subject to the elective regime under s 366A of the Act, which is discussed below, every company is in each year required to hold a general meeting as its annual general meeting. This is provided for in s 366(1), where it is further provided that the annual general meeting must be in addition to any other meetings in the year and shall be specified as the annual general meeting in the notice calling it. Section 366(3) provides that not more than 15 months shall elapse between the date of one annual general meeting of the company and that of the next. However, a relaxation is made by s 366(2) so that as long as a company holds its first annual general meeting within 18 months of its incorporation, it need not hold it in the year of its incorporation nor in the following year. Failure to comply with these provisions on the holding of meetings will, according to s 366(4), render the company and each of its officers in default liable to a fine.

The elective regime for private companies, which was introduced into the 1985 legislation, allows private companies to dispense with the holding of annual general meetings.[1] The provisions of s 366A, which allow private companies to escape the requirements in s 366, require a private company to pass an elective resolution in order to dispense with the holding of annual general meetings. The requirements for the passing of an elective resolution are laid down in s 379A. These requirements are discussed in Chapter 3.

Leaving aside the case of a private company which has elected to dispense with annual general meetings under s 366A, if an annual general meeting is not held in compliance with s 366 the Secretary of State may, on the application of a member, direct the calling of a general meeting.[2] Such a meeting is, subject to any directions given by the Secretary of State, to be regarded as an annual general meeting. If, through default in holding a meeting in one year, the Secretary of State orders a meeting to be held and it is so held in the following year, the meeting is not to be

---

1   For the definition of 'private company', see s 1(3) of the Companies Act 1985.
2   Ibid, s 367(1).

treated as the annual general meeting for the year in which it is held unless at that meeting it is so resolved.[3] Default in complying with any directions given by the Secretary of State with respect to the holding of meetings renders the company and every officer in default liable to a fine.[4]

The articles may specify what is to be usual business at an annual general meeting. However, Table A contains no such provision. Where there is no such provision then it is likely that all business must be treated as special business. The consequence of this is that no business may be transacted without previous notice of its general nature being given to members.[5] There was such a provision in reg 52 of Table A of the Companies Act 1948. The 1948 Table A may still apply to companies incorporated whilst that version of Table A was in force, if those companies have not adopted new articles since their incorporation. This regulation provides that all business transacted at an annual general meeting or an extraordinary general meeting is deemed to be special, with the exception of declaring a dividend, the consideration of the accounts and balance sheets, the consideration of the reports of the directors and auditors, the election of directors in the place of those retiring, and the appointment of, and fixing of the remuneration of, the auditors. If reg 52 of the 1948 Table A, or a like article, applies, such business may be transacted at the annual general meeting without notice of it being included in the notice of the annual general meeting.

The appointment of auditors is a matter with which every company is required to deal at each general meeting before which accounts are laid. The auditor or auditors so appointed then hold office until the conclusion of the next such meeting.[6] The provisions on the appointment of auditors are part of a code designed to buttress the independence of auditors and are considered in more detail in Chapter 3. However, the requirement to reappoint the auditor annually can be dispensed with by elective resolution. This is also dealt with in Chapter 3.

In addition to those matters required by the articles of association and the Act to be dealt with at annual general meetings, s 376(6) provides that the business of an annual general meeting includes resolutions proposed by members under s 376. This section permits members holding one-twentieth or more of the total voting rights or at least 100 members of the company, holding shares paid up to an average sum of at least £100, to require the company, at the expense of the requisitioning members, to give all members notice of resolutions proposed to be moved and also to circulate to members a statement in support of that resolution of not more than 1000 words.

---

3   Companies Act 1985, 367(4).
4   Ibid, s 367(3).
5   *R v Hill* (1825) 4 B&C 444.
6   Companies Act 1985, s 385(2).

In the absence of fraud, the directors have a right to select the place of meetings.[7] The power of the directors to select the place of meetings is a fiduciary power which must be exercised in the interests of the company. If it were called at a place or time which would be inconvenient for members so as to have the effect of restricting the attendance, this would be a wrongful exercise of their power, and could be challenged.[8]

During the whole of the annual general meeting the register of the interests of directors of the company in shares or debentures of the company and related companies required to be kept by s 325 of the Act is by reg 29 of Sch 13, Part IV of the Act required to be open to the inspection of the members. It must also be produced at the commencement of the meeting.

EXTRAORDINARY GENERAL MEETINGS

General meetings of the members other than annual general meetings, are called extraordinary general meetings (reg 36 of Table A). These meetings are held for the transaction of business by the members which cannot wait until the next annual general meeting.[9] They will usually be convened by the directors when they think proper (reg 37). They may also be called by any member or any director if there are too few directors in the UK to call a meeting (reg 37).

Under s 368, which expressly overrides any contrary provision in the articles, the directors must call a meeting on the requisition of members holding not less than one-tenth of such of the paid up capital as carries the right of voting at general meetings (or if the company has no share capital, of members representing not less than one-tenth of the voting rights of all members having the right to vote at general meetings). The requisition must state the objects of the meeting, and it must be signed by the requisitionists and deposited at the company's registered office. For this purpose, it is generally accepted in practice that a requisition sent through the post is due compliance with the requirement to deposit. The requisition may consist of several documents, each signed by one or more requisitionists (s 368(3)). Where several documents are used for the requisition, they must be in like form. This requirement does not mean they must be in exactly the same form.[10] Where a requisition is made by holders of shares held jointly, such requisition must be signed by all the joint holders.[11] See Appendix 1 for a precedent.

---

7   *Martin v Walker* (1918) 145 LTN 377.
8   *Cannon v Trask* (1875) LR 20 Eq 669.
9   The directors of a public company the net assets of which fall to one half or less of its called-up share capital must call an extraordinary general meeting: s 143 of the Companies Act 1985.
10   *Fruit and Vegetable Growers' Association v Kekewich* [1912] 2 Ch 52.
11   *Patent Wood Keg Syndicate v Pearse* (1906) WN 164.

Section 368(4) provides that if the directors do not proceed within 21 days to convene a meeting to be held within 28 days from the date of the notice convening the meeting, then those representing at least half the total voting rights of the requisitionists may proceed themselves to convene a meeting (s 368(4) and (8)). The requirement that the directors must convene the meeting for a date within 28 days from the date of the notice convening the meeting (which must be given within 21 days from the date of the deposit of the requisition) was only added in the Companies Act 1989. There is a curious mismatch between this provision and reg 37 of Table A which requires the directors to convene a meeting pursuant to a requisition within eight weeks of the date of the receipt of the requisition. It is the case, nevertheless, that the provisions of the Act should be taken to prevail.

A meeting convened by the requisitionists as a result of the directors' failure duly to proceed to convene a meeting may not be held after the expiration of three months from the date of the deposit of the requisition. When requisitioning a meeting, the requisitionists must do so in the same manner, as nearly as possible, as that in which meetings are convened by the directors (s 368(5)). The company must pay the reasonable expenses of requisitionists incurred as a result of convening a meeting, but may deduct the same amount from remuneration falling due to the defaulting directors (s 368(6)). The requisitionists are also entitled to convene a meeting where the directors convene a meeting to deal with part only of the business specified in the requisition. In this case the requisitionists may convene a meeting only for the purpose of considering the business omitted from the notice sent out by the directors.[12] Presumably, in order to convene such a meeting to deal with the business omitted from the notice sent out by the directors, those representing at least half of the total voting rights of the requisitionists must be involved in the convening of the meeting. Finally, it should be noted that any director of the company or any voting member of the company is entitled to apply to the court under s 371 for an order requiring the holding of a meeting. Where the court makes such an order the meeting must be held and conducted in the manner which the court thinks fit.

The only person other than the directors or members entitled to require the holding of an extraordinary general meeting is a resigning auditor. Pursuant to s 392A, where an auditor's notice of resignation is accompanied by a statement of circumstances which, in the auditor's opinion, should be brought to the attention of members or company creditors, then the auditor may requisition the directors to convene an extraordinary general meeting. The purpose of holding such a meeting will be to allow the meeting to receive information about and consider the circumstances which have given rise to the auditor's concern (s 392A(2)). The auditor may request the company to circulate to its members a statement in writing concerning the circumstances connected with his or her resignation. Such a statement should be circulated before the relevant meeting (s 392A(3)). The

---

12   *Isle of Wight Railway Co v Tahourdin* (1883) 25 ChD 320.

directors must convene a meeting within 21 days, to be held before the end of 28 days from the date of the notice convening the meeting. Any director who fails to take reasonable steps to secure the convening of such a meeting is guilty of an offence (s 392A(5)). Unless the auditor's statement to the members is received too late, the notice convening the meeting should indicate that such a statement has been made and a copy should be sent to every member of the company who is entitled to receive notices convening meetings (s 392A(4)). If, for any reason, every member of the company does not receive a copy of the resigning auditor's notice then the auditor is entitled to require the statement to be read out at the meeting (s 392A(6)). The right of a resigning auditor to have the contents of their statement made known to the members is subject to the ability of the company or any aggrieved person to apply to the court on the basis that the rights are 'being abused to secure needless publicity for defamatory matter'. Where such an application is made the court may order the auditor to pay the company's costs in part or in full (s 392A(7)). The provisions concerning resigning auditors are part of a more general series of provisions which are designed to strengthen the position of the company auditor. These provisions are further considered in Chapter 3.

CLASS MEETINGS

(1) Under the Companies Act 1985

The capital of a company may be divided into classes of shares with different rights, whether as to dividend, capital or voting. Different classes may be created by the memorandum, the articles, the terms of issue of shares or by the terms of the resolution authorising the issue. However, best practice is to include share rights in the articles. Rights of redemption *must* be included in the articles. The articles will often provide the conditions which must be fulfilled for the valid alteration of the rights attached to a class. It should, however, be noted that the standard set of articles contained in Table A contains no such provision. Rather, a complete code on the variation of class rights is contained in Chapter II of Part V of the Companies Act. Section 125 is the central provision of this code. It makes provision for the following four situations.

(a) Where there are class rights, however conferred, and the articles make provision for the variation of those rights provided that the variation is not concerned with authority for allotment under s 80 or a reduction of share capital under s 135
In this case, s 125(4) provides that, as long as the provision in the articles with respect to variation was included at the time of the company's original incorporation, the rights may only be varied in accordance with the provisions in the article.

(b) Where there are class rights, however conferred, and the memorandum or articles make provision for the variation of those rights and the proposed variation is in relation to an authority for allotment under s 80 or a reduction of share capital under s 135

In this situation, s 125(3) provides that the class rights may only be varied if either the holders of 75 per cent in nominal value of the issued shares of that class consent in writing or the variation is sanctioned by an extraordinary resolution at a meeting of the holders of that class of shares. If the memorandum or articles provide further requirements for variation in this context then compliance with those requirements is also necessary.

(c) Where rights are conferred in the memorandum and neither the memorandum nor the articles make provisions with respect to variation of those rights

In this situation, s 125(5) provides that the class rights may only be varied if all members of the company agree to the variation.

(d) Where the class rights are attached otherwise than by the memorandum and the articles make no provision with respect to variation of those rights

In this situation, s 125(2) provides that the class rights may only be varied if either the holders of 75 per cent in nominal value of the issued shares of that class consent in writing, or an extraordinary resolution is passed at a class meeting of the holders of that class. If there is any other requirement for variation in this situation, however imposed, compliance with this must also take place.

For the purposes of the application of s 125, it should be noted that an alteration of a provision in the articles for variation of class rights is itself a variation of those rights (s 125(7)) and an abrogation of class rights is also to be treated as a variation (s 125(8)).

Where the above rules as to variation of class rights require the holding of a meeting, then s 125(6) makes the requirements of s 369 as to the length of notice for calling company meetings, the requirements of s 370 as to meetings and votes, and the requirements of ss 376 and 377 as to circulation of members' resolutions, as well as any provisions in the articles relating to general meetings, so far as applicable, relevant. This is subject to two conditions: first, at any meeting other than an adjourned meeting, the quorum is two persons holding at least one-third of the nominal value of the issued shares of the relevant class (at an adjourned meeting the quorum is one person holding shares of the relevant class); and, secondly, any holders of shares in the relevant class may demand a poll. However, it should be noted that where the articles make detailed provisions as to the conduct of class meetings, these probably override the provisions of s 125(6). This is a vexed point and it may be wise to ensure that the two qualifications regarding quorum and a poll are complied with in any case. (The provisions of s 369 on notice for calling company meetings including notice for members' resolutions and s 370 on meetings and votes are discussed in Chapters 5 and 6 respectively.)

(2) On the directions of the court pursuant to s 425

The meetings referred to above are convened by the company in the same way as meetings of the company are convened, but there is another kind of class meeting which may be held. This is under s 425. Under this section, where a compromise or arrangement is proposed between a company and its creditors or any class of them or between the company and its members or any class of them, the court may, on the application of the company or of any creditor or member of the company, or, in the case of a company being wound up or subject to an administration order, of the liquidator or the administrator, order a meeting of the creditors or class of creditors, or of the members of the company or class of members, as the case may be, to be summoned in such manner as the court directs. If a majority in number representing three-fourths in value of the creditors or class of creditors or members or class of members, as the case may be, present and voting either in person or by proxy at the meeting, agree to any compromise or arrangement, the compromise or arrangement, if sanctioned by the court, becomes binding on all the creditors or the class of creditors, or on the members or class of members, as the case may be, and also on the company or, in the case of a company in the course of being wound up, on the liquidator and contributories of the company. (The expression 'arrangement' includes a reorganisation of the share capital of the company by the consolidation of shares of different classes or by the division of shares into shares of different classes or by both those methods (s 425(6)(b)).) A 'compromise or arrangement' may include a complete change in the company's capital structure, and may even amount to its acquisition by another company.[13] In the latter case, however, the court will impose a heavy burden on those who support the scheme to show that it is a fair one.[14]

Pursuant to s 426, a company proposing a scheme of arrangement under s 425 is required to give certain specified information regarding the effect of the scheme and the interests of directors and debenture stock trustees. This information must be contained in a statement which must accompany every notice summoning the required meeting under s 425. Failure to provide such a statement makes the company and every defaulting officer liable to a fine. Liquidators, administrators and trustees under a debenture trust deed are deemed to be officers for this purpose (s 426(6)). It should, however, be noted that mere compliance with the statutory requirement as to what must be disclosed in this statement may not be sufficient to ensure the court's sanction of the scheme. In particular, if there has been a subsequent change in the directors' material interests which is not disclosed to or

---

13   *Re National Bank Ltd* [1966] 1 WLR 819.
14   *Re Hellenic & General Trust Ltd* [1976] 1 WLR 123.

before the relevant meeting the court will need to be satisfied that no reasonable person would have changed their mind and their vote in the light of that information before it will sanction the scheme of arrangement.[15]

Section 425 is a useful provision enabling all the members and creditors to be bound by a scheme of which the majorities of the various classes approve. Sometimes difficult questions as to what constitutes a separate class for the purposes of the section are raised. Generally speaking, if either:

(a)   certain shares have different rights from other shares, and those rights are relevant for consideration of the scheme; or
(b)   certain shares are treated differently under the scheme from others,

then separate classes exist for the purpose of the section. It was certainly once thought that a single type of share with similar rights and which was to be treated uniformly by the scheme constituted a single and indivisible class.[16] In *Re Hellenic & General Trust Ltd*,[17] however, a single shareholder with 53 per cent of the shares was the subsidiary of the bank which would, under the scheme, obtain all the new ordinary shares to be issued by the company (the old shares being cancelled in return for cash compensation). It was held that the subsidiary had an interest in the 'purchaser's camp' distinct from the interest of the other shareholders. Consequently, the subsidiary formed a separate class, so that separate class meetings should have been held to approve the scheme. It is generally thought that the decision somewhat strains the meaning of 'class rights' and it seems that this notion of class rights should be confined strictly to the rules on schemes of arrangement under s 425. The case is unlikely to be treated as good authority in respect of any more general definition of class rights.

The meetings for the purpose of consenting to a scheme of arrangement are summoned by the order of the court and in accordance with its directions. Failure to comply with the court's directions may result in the court refusing to sanction the scheme.[18] Proxies may be used in meetings under s 425, provided the company is not in liquidation.[19] The form of a proxy for these purposes will be settled in chambers. Directors who hold proxies for or against a scheme must use them.[20]

The class meetings themselves do not constitute general meetings of the company. If the scheme requires either the consent of the company in general meeting, or some corporate act which has to be performed in general meeting, such as an

---

15   *Re Minster Assets plc* [1985] BCLC 200.
16   *Re Alabama, New Orleans, Texas & Pacific Junction Railway* [1891] 1 Ch 213. 'Classes' of creditors may be a more flexible concept. For example, holders of matured insurance policies constitute a class separate from other policy-holders; *Sovereign Life Assurance Co v Dodd* [1892] 2 QB 573.
17   [1976] 1 WLR 123.
18   Cf *Re Anglo-Spanish Tartar Refineries* [1924] WN 222.
19   *Re Magadi Soda Co* [1925] WN 50.
20   *Re Dorman, Long & Co* [1934] Ch 635.

increase or reduction of capital, then an extraordinary general meeting must be convened for this purpose. Such a meeting is convened by the directors in the ordinary way, and is not called on the direction of the court. Proxies for such general meeting must follow the form required by the articles. On proxies, see Chapter 9.

(3) In relation to compensation to directors for loss of office

As to class meetings that may be required to be held in connection with compensation to directors for loss of office, see Chapter 5.

MEETINGS OF DEBENTURE STOCKHOLDERS

Akin to class meetings are meetings of debenture stockholders. These will be convened and conducted in accordance with the provisions contained in the debenture stock trust deed. Under trust deeds made some years ago, the provisions for calling meetings of debenture stockholders are often inadequate for modern requirements. The quorum requirements are often so high that in practice they are difficult to attain, and these requirements often extend through to a meeting adjourned from the original date, through lack of quorum, to a later date. A second defect is often the very restricted powers for amendment of the deed; frequently, they cannot be used to enable the substitution of a similar debenture stock of another company in place of that under the trust deed. Such substitution is often very desirable in the case of a takeover bid for the company concerned, or if the parent company in a group wishes to rationalise the financial structure and borrowing of the group.

If the provisions under the trust deed are inadequate, the company has to have recourse to a scheme under s 425.

Where a meeting of debenture holders is held, each holder may vote in his or her own interests, but if the holder has conflicting interests in a capacity as member of the company, or as a creditor of a different class, he or she must not vote in favour of the other interest, or, if he or she does, his or her vote may be open to challenge.[21]

A person may be entitled to vote at a meeting of debenture holders if debentures have been allotted to him or her, his or her name is in the register of debenture holders, and he or she has the right to call for duly sealed debentures and is bound to accept them.[22]

Debentures are often issued on the terms that the rights of the holders may be varied with the consent of a certain proportion of the holders or with the consent of

---

21 *Re New York Taxi Cab Co* [1913] 1 Ch 1.
22 *Dey v Rubber & Mercantile Corporation* [1923] 2 Ch 528.

a resolution passed by a particular majority at a meeting of the holders. Any such variation must, to be valid, be strictly in accordance with the terms of the debentures. A power of this kind to vary rights will not justify abandoning rights and a power to compromise can only be exercised if there is some dispute to compromise,[23] or if there is some compromise (but not abandonment) of rights.[24] Where there is no power to compromise then, in order to achieve a compromise, it will be necessary to resort to s 425.

---

23   *Mercantile Investment Co v International Co of Mexico* [1893] 1 Ch 484n.
24   *Re NFU Development Trust Ltd* [1972] 1 WLR 1548.

Chapter 5

NOTICE OF MEMBERS' MEETINGS

INTRODUCTION

Where all the members of a company entitled to be present at a meeting agree on a particular course proposed then, provided the matter is within the power of the general meeting, this will constitute a valid corporate act. The law which permits this is known as the doctrine of informal corporate acts,[1] and it is now supplemented by provisions in ss 381A to 381C on written resolutions of members of private companies in lieu of a meeting. Both these matters were considered in Chapter 3. In the absence, however, of an informal corporate act or a written resolution under the provisions of ss 381A to 381C, the company will only be validly assembled so as to be able to transact business where a meeting is convened by a proper notice given in accordance with the provisions of the Act and the company's articles. Generally, the notice must be written, must state the time and place of the meeting, and the nature of the business to be transacted except where such business is of a kind for which notice is not required under the articles. Consistent with the doctrine of informal corporate acts, however, any defect in notice will be cured if all the members entitled to be present at the meeting attend and agree on the course proposed.[2]

PERIOD OF NOTICE

The articles generally provide for a certain length of notice. Section 369(1), however, provides that any provision in the articles which allows for the calling of a meeting, except an adjourned meeting, on shorter notice than the period specified in that subsection, is void. The periods of notice specified are 21 days' notice in writing for an annual general meeting; or, in the case of a meeting which is not an annual general meeting or at which it is not proposed to pass a special resolution, seven days' notice in writing for an unlimited company or 14 days' notice in writing for any other company. Ordinary and extraordinary resolutions of a limited company therefore require 14 days' notice unless the articles specify a longer

---

1   *Parker & Cooper v Reading* [1926] 1 Ch 975; *Re Duomatic Ltd* [1969] 2 WLR 114; *Cane v Jones* [1980] 1 WLR 1451.
2   *Baroness Wenlock v River Dee Co* (1883) 36 ChD 681n.

period. One instance in which articles do require a longer period is reg 38 in Table A which requires 21 days' notice for a resolution appointing a person as a director at a general meeting. Where the articles are void as a result of contravening s 369(1), or are silent as to the period of notice, then these specified periods of notice will apply (s 369(2)). So far as the period of notice for a meeting at which a special resolution is to be proposed is concerned, s 378(2) provides for a period of 21 days' notice.

Periods of notice shorter than those stipulated in the Act or in the articles may be given in the following circumstances. In the case of an annual general meeting, short notice may be given if agreed to by all the members entitled to attend and vote (s 369(3)). In any other case, short notice may be given if agreed to by a majority in number of such members having between them 95 per cent in nominal value of the total voting rights at the meeting (ss 369(3) and (4), and 378(3)). It should, however, be noted that as a result of the introduction of the elective regime for private companies in the Companies Act 1989, a private company may elect to allow short notice with the consent of at least 90 per cent in nominal value of the total voting rights at the meeting (ss 369(4) and 378(3)). Such an election will only be effective if passed in accordance with the regime for elective resolutions in s 379A. This regime is considered in Chapter 3.

The number of days' notice must be clear.[3] This means that in calculating whether the period of notice has been given, the day upon which the notice is given or is deemed to be given and the day upon which the meeting is to be held must be excluded. Table A, reg 115 provides that notices are deemed to have been given 48 hours after they have been posted. Reliance on this provision, however, during a postal strike may be a ground for the grant of an injunction to a member, who did not receive the notice in good time, to restrain the holding of the meeting.[4]

THE PROPER AUTHORITY FOR THE ISSUE OF NOTICES

It is usually the directors who are responsible for convening the annual general meeting and empowered to convene extraordinary meetings (see, for example, Table A, reg 37). This power to convene meetings is a power of the board, not of only some of the directors[5] (unless acting as a duly appointed committee with power to convene meetings).

---

3   *Mercantile Co v International Co of Mexico* [1893] 1 Ch 484n; *Re Hector Whaling Co* [1936] Ch 208; and see, for example, Table A, reg 38.
4   *Bradman v Trinity Estates plc* [1989] BCLC 757.
5   *Browne v La Trinidad* (1887) 37 ChD 1, 17.

A notice issued by the secretary without the authority of a resolution of the directors duly assembled at a board meeting is invalid,[6] and where a meeting is requisitioned under s 368 the secretary cannot validly summon a meeting without the authority of the board of directors.[7] A notice issued without such authority, either because no instructions have been given by the board for its issue or because the instructions were given by an improperly constituted board, may become a good notice if adopted and ratified by a proper board meeting held prior to the general meeting. As was said in *Hooper v Kerr*:

'The question is whether, although the notice was not authorised beforehand, it has been so ratified now as to make it a good and valid notice . . . The principle of the cases . . . is that the ratification of an act purporting to be done by an agent on your behalf dates back to the performance of the act.'[8]

In this context, note should also be taken of Table A, reg 92, which provides that all acts done by any meeting of directors, a committee of directors or by any person acting as a director shall, notwithstanding that it be afterwards discovered that there was some defect in the appointment of any such director or that they or any of them were disqualified, had vacated office, or were otherwise not entitled to vote, be valid as if every such person had been duly appointed, was qualified to be a director and entitled to vote. An article in this form may validate a meeting held on notices sent out by an irregularly constituted board.[9] As to the extent to which such an article will be effective, see *Morris v Kanssen*.[10]

Notices should be signed by the secretary, qualified by the words 'By Order of the Board', and the secretary should see that the board meeting, which has authorised the convening of a general meeting, was itself properly convened and that a quorum of directors was present. Where, however, the articles make no provision for the calling of meetings, two or more members holding not less than one-tenth of the issued share capital, or if the company does not have a share capital, not less than five per cent in number of the members of the company, may call a meeting (s 370(3)).

As to the powers of members to give notice of a meeting in certain circumstances, see Chapter 2.

In the case of a company limited by shares any member of the company entitled to attend and vote at a meeting of it is entitled to appoint another person as his or her proxy to attend and vote instead of him or her. The proxy need not be a member of

---

6   *Re Haycroft Gold Reduction Co* [1900] 2 Ch 230.
7   *Re State of Wyoming Syndicate* [1901] 2 Ch 431; and see also s 368 of the Companies Act 1985.
8   (1900) 83 LT 730.
9   *Transport Ltd v Schomburg* (1905) 21 TLR 305.
10 [1946] AC 459.

the company. A statement to that effect must appear 'with reasonable prominence' on every notice calling a general meeting (s 372(1) and (3)).

If the articles allow a member to appoint one or more proxies (as reg 59 in Table A does), the statement must include a reference to that right.

In the case of a company limited by guarantee there is no right to appoint a proxy unless the articles so provide. If the articles do so provide they can also require that a proxy must be an existing member. There is no requirement to include a statement on each notice to inform members of a guarantee company of their rights but it is good practice to include one.

TO WHOM NOTICES SHOULD BE SENT

(a) Members
Subject to any limitations in the articles, all members on the register are entitled to receive notice of meetings,[11] and if notice is not sent to any person entitled to receive it, the meeting is irregular and its proceedings invalid.[12] Articles normally provide that accidental failure to give notice will not invalidate a meeting or the proceedings.[13] However, if the failure to send a notice is deliberate, for example where the company believes that notice to the address in a register will not reach the member and accordingly does not send one to that member, the saving of the article will not operate as the failure to send the notice is not accidental.[14]

(b) Special classes of members
Articles often prescribe that certain classes of members shall not be entitled to receive notice. An example of such a class are the holders of preference shares in cases where the preference shares do not confer the right to vote. If the preference shares do not confer the right to vote, but the articles make no special provision on notice, it is unclear whether the preference shareholders will be entitled to notice.[15] To exclude all doubt, articles which provide that certain classes of members are not to have a vote also often provide that they shall not be entitled to receive notices of or to attend meetings.

---

11 Companies Act 1985, s 370(2) and Table A, reg 38.
12 *Smyth v Darley* (1849) 2 HLC 789. Note also that in *Re A Company (No 00789 of 1987), ex parte Shooter* [1990] BCLC 384, it was held that the holding of an extraordinary general meeting without adequate notice, at which new shares were created, was grounds for a petition alleging unfairly prejudicial conduct under s 459 of the Companies Act 1995.
13 *Re West Canadian Collieries* [1962] Ch 370; Table A, reg 39.
14 *Musselwhite v C H Musselwhite* [1962] Ch 964.
15 *Re Mackenzie* [1916] 2 Ch 450; *Re Warden & Hotchkiss* [1945] Ch 270, 278, but see s 370(2) of the Companies Act 1985.

(c) Joint holders of shares

All joint holders must be given notice individually unless the articles, as they almost invariably do, provide that this shall not be necessary. Regulation 112 of Table A, for example, provides that notice to all joint holders may be given to the first-named joint holder in the register.

(d) Persons entitled to a share as a result of the death or bankruptcy of a member

In the absence of any provision in the articles, persons who become entitled to a share as a result of the death or bankruptcy of a member are not automatically entitled to notice of meetings, because they are not members of the company. It is common, however, for articles to provide, as does reg 38 of Table A, that notice be given to a person entitled to a share as a result of the death or bankruptcy of a member. It is unclear what such people should do with this notice since reg 31 of Table A provides that, before being registered as the holder of a share, a person entitled to a share as a result of death or bankruptcy is not entitled to attend or vote at any meeting of the company. To avoid this peculiar result, companies may well choose to diverge from the provisions of Table A and provide that notice need not be given to persons entitled to a share as a result of death or bankruptcy.

It should be noted in this context that a member who becomes bankrupt remains a member and is able to exercise the votes attached to his or her shares, notwithstanding that by taking appropriate steps under the appropriate provisions the trustee in bankruptcy might be able to secure registration as the holder of the shares.[16] A company cannot, therefore, treat a member who is known to be bankrupt in any other manner than they treat other members, whether in connection with sending notices to that member or accepting the votes of that member.

(e) Directors

Articles commonly require that notice of meetings be given to the directors. Regulation 38 of Table A is an example of such an article.

(f) Auditors

The auditor is entitled to attend any general meeting and to receive all notices and other communications relating to such a meeting (s 391(a) and (b)). The auditor is also entitled to be heard on any part of the business affecting him or her as auditor (s 390(1)(c)).

(g) Debenture holders

As a result of a special provision in s 5(8), notice of a special resolution to alter the objects clause of a company's memorandum must be given not only to members, but also to holders of any debentures secured by a floating charge issued or first

---

16   *Morgan & Gray* [1953] Ch 83.

issued before 1 December 1947 or debentures which form part of the same series as any debentures so issued. The subsection requires the same notice to be given to debenture holders as is given to members of the company. The provision does not confer on relevant debenture holders the right to attend the meeting, rather its purpose is to give them the right to object to the alteration.

Provision can be made in, or authorised by, a company's articles for notice to be given by advertisement in some instances. Such advertisement may be required to be inserted in a particular newspaper or posted in some specified place. If the requirements are complied with, the notice is duly given. This is, however, unusual except in cases where the persons entitled to notice are unknown such as holders of bearer warrants or untraced members. In the former instance the relevant provisions are invariably included in the terms of issue of the bearer warrants and printed on the reverse of each. In the latter instance they are invariably included in the articles.

METHOD OF SERVICE

Articles usually provide for the method of serving notices on the members and compliance with any method prescribed in the articles is necessary. If, for example, the articles require notice through the post and notice is, in fact, given in a newspaper advertisement, such notice would be irregular, and vice versa. It should be noted, however, that if a meeting is irregularly convened, a person who attends and takes part may be unable subsequently to complain of the irregularity. For example, at an adjourned general meeting, notice of which adjournment was given by circulars sent to shareholders but not by advertisement as required by the deed of settlement, it was resolved to make a call. A shareholder who was present and voted at the adjourned meeting was not entitled to take advantage of the irregularity of the notice.[17]

Insofar as the articles do not make any provision for service of notices of meetings, every such notice must be served on every member of the company (not merely those entitled to vote) in the manner in which notices are required to be served by the Table A for the time being in force (s 370(2)). These provisions are now found in regs 111 to 116 of Table A. Regulation 111 provides that notice for a company meeting shall be in writing. Regulation 112 provides that notice may be given to a member personally, by post or by leaving it at the registered address of the member. Where the notices are to be given by post, then reg 115 provides that the notice is deemed to have been given at the expiration of 48 hours after the envelope was posted. The same regulation further provides that it shall be conclusive evidence that notice was given if it was proved that an envelope containing the notice was properly addressed, stamped and posted.

---

17   *Re British Sugar Refinery Co* [1857] 26 LJ Ch 369.

An important feature of the regulations on notice in Table A is the provision which entitles a member whose registered address is outside the UK to have notices given at a stipulated address within the UK. The regulation goes on to provide, however, that if such a member does not provide a UK address, he or she will have no entitlement to receive any notices from the company (reg 112). The equivalent regulation in Table A to the 1948 Act was the subject of *Parkstone Ltd v Gulf Guarantee Bank plc.*[18] In this case, a member with an address in Gibraltar had also given the company an address in the UK for the service of notices. The company, however, sent a notice to the address in Gibraltar. The court held that this was a valid notice under reg 131 of the 1948 Table A. It seems unlikely that a similar result would have been produced on these facts if the regulation in question had been in the form of reg 112 of the present Table A. This is because reg 112, unlike the old reg 131, 'entitles' members to have notices given to them at their stipulated UK address.

In *Re Warden & Hotchkiss Ltd,*[19] it was held that where the articles do not provide (as Table A does) that notice need not be given to members whose only address is outside the UK but do provide that a notice will be deemed to be delivered when the letter containing it would have been delivered in the ordinary course of post, then notice need not be given to members with registered addresses abroad. It seems, however, that this decision should now be regarded as applying only to companies whose articles are in exactly the same form as those in Table A to the 1862 Act. In other cases, a reference to the ordinary course of post should not be construed as including only post within the UK.[20]

Of course, it is open to members of a company to alter the articles by special resolution to provide that members with an overseas address are entitled to notice at that address. It may also be sensible in such a case to alter articles (such as reg 115 in Table A) governing the deemed date of service of notices sent by post.

Persons situated abroad who do not have the right to receive notices to company meetings are those persons who are enemies or who are situated in enemy territory. The right of such people to receive notices is suspended so long as they remain an enemy or in enemy territory, and meetings are properly convened though no notice has been served upon a person who, if not an enemy, would be entitled to notice.[21]

---

18 [1990] TLR 477.
19 [1945] Ch 270.
20 *Parkstone Ltd v Gulf Guarantee Bank plc* [1990] TLR 477.
21 *Re Anglo-International Bank* [1943] Ch 233.

TIME AND PLACE OF MEETING

The notice must state the time and place of the meeting. The fixing of these is usually left by the articles to the discretion of the directors (see, for example, reg 38 of Table A); however, they must be reasonably convenient for the shareholders.

Although the court will not usually interfere with the powers and duties of directors in their management of the internal affairs of a company, directors will be restrained from fixing a particular date for holding the annual general meeting of the company for the purpose of preventing members from exercising their voting powers.[22]

THE REAL NATURE OF THE BUSINESS TO BE TRANSACTED

The vote of the majority at a general meeting, as it binds both dissentient and absent members, must be a vote given on proper information. This is consistent with the general principle that matters must be fairly put before the meeting and the meeting itself must be conducted in the fairest possible manner.[23]

The notice of an annual general meeting is not required to specify any business unless that business is declared by the articles to be special business. Subject to this principle, the notice for any company meeting must give a fair, candid and reasonable explanation of the business intended to be transacted.[24] The test, which is admittedly an extremely imprecise one, is that the notice should be in sufficient detail and of sufficient clarity for a member reading it to be able to determine whether he or she should attend the meeting and if necessary ask questions, or whether the member may without concern allow the meeting to pass the resolution without his or her attendance or enquiry. This test will certainly not be satisfied if the notice merely says that details or copies of resolutions may be seen at the company's offices or that copies will be forwarded on request.[25] Giving facilities for obtaining information is not equivalent to giving the information.

It is sometimes found that, rather than attempt to summarise particularly complex proposals or changes, companies will set out in full the relevant provisions, often by way of an appendix. This procedure does not seem to be a proper course for directors to follow. Even though it may contain all the relevant material, it will be in so indigestible a form as to be an unfair presentation. The proper procedure is for the notice to summarise the proposals and, if these involve changes from existing

---

22   *Cannon v Trask* (1875) LR 20 Eq 669.
23   *Tiessen v Henderson* [1899] 1 Ch 861.
24   *Kaye v Croydon Tramways* [1898] 1 Ch 358.
25   *Normandy v Ind Coope & Co* [1908] 1 Ch 84.

provisions, to summarise the differences. Members may then be offered the full details for inspection on request, but they will at least know what they are seeking. Such a procedure is often disliked by directors, who feel cautious lest some provision may unwittingly be summarised incorrectly or overlooked, but the information is more likely to be presented clearly using this procedure.

Notice of an annual general meeting must specify the meeting as such (s 366(1)), and when it is proposed to pass a special or extraordinary resolution at any meeting, the notice of the meeting must specify that the resolution is to be passed as a special or extraordinary resolution, as the case may be (s 378). Since this intention must be specified in relation to 'the resolution', the text of the resolution or its entire substance must be set out in the notice. There is no point in adding to the notice words such as 'with such amendments and alterations as may be determined at the meeting', because no amendment may be made to any such proposed resolution. If the resolution as passed is different from that specified in the notice, notice of intention to propose the resolution actually passed will not have been given as required by s 378, and it will therefore not be a special or extraordinary resolution, even if passed by the required majority.[26] On the other hand, if the irregularity is a mere typographical error or other slip which would be obvious in the light of the proposal and the information given, the resolution may be passed in its proper form and will be effective; it is not necessary to reconvene the meeting. The courts have, on various occasions, acted on this principle when confirming reductions of capital.

An ordinary resolution need not be passed in the exact terms of the notice, and under all ordinary forms of articles there is no need to specify a proposed ordinary resolution.[27] It is sufficient to specify the nature of the business. In *Betts & Co v MacNaghten*[28] the notice stated that the meeting was for the purpose of considering the following resolution with such amendments and alterations as should be determined upon at that meeting, 'That A, B, and C be appointed directors'. The notice was taken as read at the meeting and A, B, C and two other persons were appointed directors. It was held that the notice sufficiently indicated the special business to be transacted, and that the particularity of the names did not put greater restriction upon the meeting than there would have been had the notice been in general terms; and accordingly all five were properly appointed. So, too, an amendment to an ordinary resolution which has been set out in the notice will not invalidate the resolution. But this will only apply if the amendment renders the resolution less, and not more, onerous to the company or its members, for example where the remuneration to be paid to directors is, under the amended resolution,

---

26 *MacConnell v Prill & Co* [1916] 2 Ch 57. But the members may agree to waive their rights to notice in accordance with s 369(3) (extraordinary resolutions) or s 378(3) (special resolutions) of the Companies Act 1985.

27 Unless it is one of which special notice is required under ibid, s 379. This is discussed further in Chapter 3.

28 [1910] 1 Ch 430.

less than that proposed in the notice.[29] The reason for this is that shareholders may have given proxies, or desisted from voting, because they were content with the stated proposal, but might have had a different attitude had the more onerous proposal been proposed originally.

An annual general meeting may transact special business if (and only if) the notice provides for it[30] and there is nothing in the articles confining special business to extraordinary meetings. In practice, many companies convene an annual general meeting to transact the ordinary business followed by an extraordinary general meeting, on the same day, to conduct special business. At whatever type of meeting it is to be transacted, the purport of the special business must be stated in the notice convening the meeting. The transaction of that special business will otherwise be invalid.[31] (However, the transaction at a meeting of some business outside the object specified in the notice will not make the whole meeting irregular.)[32]

Where the notice deals with two separate resolutions the failure of the one will not invalidate the other, even in cases where they are closely associated.[33] If it is intended that one proposal should take effect only if another does, they should either be put in a single resolution or made interdependent in their terms.

NOTICE OF PROPOSAL TO PAY COMPENSATION TO DIRECTORS

The Act contains important provisions as to disclosing proposals to pay compensation for loss of office to directors. Under s 312, a company may not make any payment to a director in compensation for loss of office or in consideration of or in connection with his or her retirement from office unless the particulars as to the proposed payment and the amount are disclosed to the members of the company and the proposal for payment is approved by the company. Therefore, when any such payment is proposed, a meeting of the company must be held and the notice must contain the particulars required by this section. Section 313 requires similar disclosure and approval by the company of any payment made to any director of compensation for loss of office or as consideration for, or in connection with, retirement from office when any such payment is proposed to be made in connection with the transfer of the whole or any part of the undertaking

---

29 *Torbuck v Westbury (Lord)* [1902] 2 Ch 871. The resolution in this case was a special resolution, and the section of the Companies Act 1862 relating to special resolutions differed from s 378 of the Companies Act 1985.
30 *Graham v Van Diemen's Land Co* (1856) 26 LJ Ex 73.
31 *Lawes' Case* (1852) 1 De GM&G 421; *Kaye v Croydon Tramways Co* [1898] 1 Ch 358.
32 *Re British Sugar Refinery Co* (1857) 26 LJ Ch 369.
33 *Cleve v Financial Corporation* (1873) LR 16 Eq 363.

and property of the company. The section applies whether the proposed payment is by the company itself or some other person, for example a bidder for the shares. Section 314 deals with the situation when a similar payment is proposed to be made to a director in connection with transfers of shares in the company resulting from certain classes of offers to purchase the shares mentioned in the section, which include offers conditional on acceptance to a given extent. In such cases it is the duty of the director to see that the particulars and amount of the proposed payment are disclosed in the offer to purchase the shares. Section 315 provides that any such proposed payment must be approved by a meeting of the holders of all the shares to which the offer relates and of all the other shares of that class or those classes of shares. The provisions of the Act and the articles as to the holding of general meetings, apply to meetings to be held under s 315. The Secretary of State, on the application of any person concerned, may direct a modification to those usual rules for the purpose of a meeting under this section (s 315(2)). (The section itself modifies the usual rules as to the consequences of a lack of quorum (s 315(3)).)

The limitations of these sections should be noted. Section 312 deals only with compensation for loss of office as a director. It does not deal with the loss of any other position, and in particular it does not cover compensation which the company is already contractually bound to make, for example on termination of employment of its managing director.[34] Where, as will commonly be the case, the board has the power to appoint a managing director on such terms and with such remuneration as it may determine (Table A, reg 84), s 312 simply does not apply and the general meeting has no voice. Broadly the same considerations apply to the other sections.

RESOLUTION CIRCULATED ON THE REQUISITION OF MEMBERS

In the ordinary case, the business specified in the notice will be that which the convenors of the meeting think ought to be transacted. However, s 376 provides for the giving of notice of resolutions and circulation of statements relating to business proposed to be transacted at the insistence of persons other than the convenors of the meeting. It permits persons other than the convenors of the meeting, at their own expense, to require the company:

(a) to give notice of a resolution which may properly be moved and is intended to be moved at the next annual general meeting; and

(b) to circulate any statement with respect to any matter to be dealt with at any forthcoming general meeting. The statement must not be more than 1,000 words.

---

34   *Taupo Totara Timber Co Ltd v Rowe* [1978] AC 537.

The meeting itself can decide that any such notice or statement shall not be at the expense of the requisitionists. Requisitionists are therefore well advised to include in their resolutions one which puts the expenses of the requisition on the company. As appears from the foregoing summary, the requisitionists can have notice of a resolution given only for an annual general meeting. They can, however, secure the circulation of a statement relating to any proposal which is to be considered at any general meeting, whether or not an annual general meeting.

The requisition may only be given by the holders of not less than one-twentieth of the total voting rights exercisable at the meeting to which the requisition relates or by not less than 100 members holding shares in the company on which there has been paid up an average sum, per member, of not less than £100 (s 376(2)). Section 376(3), (4) and (5) provide for the method of serving the notice or statement. Section 376(3) provides that the resolution and statement should be circulated to all members of the company entitled to have notice of the meeting in the manner permitted for service of notice of the meeting. Notice of a resolution must also be given to any other member of the company by giving notice of its general effect in the manner permitted for giving notice of meetings of the company (s 376(4)). Finally, s 376(5) provides that a copy of the resolution or statement, or the notice of the effect of the resolution (under s 376(4)) should be given in the same manner and as far as practicable at the same time as the notice of the meeting. Where such notice is not given at the same time as the notice of the meeting, it should be served as soon as practicable thereafter.

Section 377 sets out the circumstances in which the company will not be obliged to circulate a resolution or a statement under s 376. These circumstances include the situation where the company or any other person who claims to be aggrieved by the terms of any such statement applies to the court and the court is satisfied that the rights conferred by the section are being abused to secure needless publicity for defamatory matter (s 377(3)).

MEETING ORDERED TO BE HELD BY THE COURT

If, for any reason, it is impracticable to call or to conduct a meeting of a company, the court may order one to be convened and held, and may give such directions as to the calling and conduct of the meeting as it thinks expedient (s 371). The directions may include a provision that one member present in person or by proxy shall constitute a meeting. The court may call a meeting notwithstanding the opposition of some members.[35] (However, it may not call a meeting where to do so would override class rights.)[36] The power under s 371 is useful if there is a dispute as to the identity of the duly constituted directors able to call a meeting. It has also

---

35   *Re El Sombrero Ltd* [1958] Ch 900.
36   *BML Group Ltd v Harman* (1994) *The Times*, April 8, CA.

recently been used to call meetings in circumstances involving a petition under s 459 that the affairs of the company have been conducted in an unfairly prejudicial manner.[37]

The extent of the court's powers under s 371 were made clear in *Re British Union for the Abolition of Vivisection*.[38] A previous extraordinary general meeting of the company had been disrupted by a minority of the members who were also on the company's 'committee' or board of directors. It was possible that the 'near riot' conditions which had prevailed at previous general meetings would deter members from attending them in future. However, the articles provided that members could not vote unless present in person. Proxies were not permitted. The articles were valid because the company was limited by guarantee (s 372(2)).

An application was made to the court under s 371 for a general meeting to be held to consider a resolution to alter the articles to allow proxy voting. The court granted the application and, addressing the concern that the disruptive element might use the same tactics as in the past to prevent the resolution being passed, the court also ordered that the general meeting should be attended only by the leaders of the disruptive minority but that the rest of the membership should be entitled to vote by postal vote.

The court's powers under s 371 were therefore exercised to override both the articles and the provisions of the Companies Act which would otherwise have applied in relation to voting procedure at general meetings.

Annual general meetings may be ordered to be held by the Secretary of State for Trade and Industry, on the requisition of any member of the company, but experience shows that it is difficult to persuade the Secretary of State to act (s 376).

AUTHENTICATION OF NOTICES

A notice must be properly authenticated. Section 41 provides that a document requiring authentication by a company may be signed by a director, secretary or other authorised officer of the company. Section 744 provides that a notice is a document for this purpose.

---

37   *Re Sticky Fingers Restaurant Ltd* [1991] BCC 754; *Re Whitchurch Insurance Consultants Ltd* [1993] BCLC 1359.
38   (1995) *The Times*, March 3.

Chapter 6

QUORUM AND APPOINTMENT OF CHAIRMAN AT GENERAL MEETINGS

QUORUM

(1) General rules

The articles generally make provision as to the number of members who constitute a quorum, that is, the number of members who are entitled to transact business of the meeting so as to bind all the members. If the articles do not lay down the number of members necessary to form a quorum at a meeting of the company, it is provided by s 370(4) that two members personally present shall be a quorum. There is an exception to this rule for single member companies incorporated under s 1(3A), which is laid down in s 370A. This section provides that for such a company, notwithstanding anything to the contrary in its articles, its quorum for meetings is one.

Only persons entitled to vote are counted in a quorum,[1] although the articles may provide that this includes persons holding a proxy for a voting member (see, for example, Table A, reg 40). If the articles so permit, a person present by proxy only may be counted towards the quorum. Usually, however, one member cannot constitute a quorum no matter how many proxies that person holds.[2] This rule is, of course, subject to an exception for single member companies, and is also subject to several other exceptions discussed below.

Articles normally state what is to happen if no quorum is present when the meeting is due to begin. An example is that found in reg 41 of Table A which provides that, if within half an hour no quorum is present, the meeting stands adjourned for one week exactly and is to be held at the same place, or at such other time and place as the directors may determine. Under reg 41, this also applies if at any time during the meeting a quorum ceases to be present. Some companies may regard this requirement for a meeting to remain quorate as inconvenient as it may permit a member who is unhappy with the progress of the meeting to bring it to a halt by walking out. Problems such as this may, to some extent, be dealt with under the principles of law preventing abuse of quorum provisions (discussed below).

---

1   *Young v South African Syndicate* [1896] 2 Ch 268; Cf *Re Greymouth-Point Elizabeth Railway Co* [1904] 1 Ch 32.
2   *Re Sanitary Carbon Co* [1877] WN 223.

Nevertheless, some companies may not wish to include this particular requirement of the present Table A in their articles. Ordinarily, the quorum for an adjourned meeting is the same as that for any other meeting (see, for example, Table A, reg 40).

A question can arise whether two joint holders, present personally or by proxy, can be counted for the purpose of a quorum, the question being due to the article normally found (see Table A, reg 55) which has the effect that the first-named in the register in respect of a holding may vote so as to exclude the votes of the other. On principle, however, the answer must be that both can be counted for a quorum as both are members and both are entitled to vote. The votes of the second-named would be excluded if the first-named were to vote all the jointly held shares, but the first-named is not bound to do that and will not necessarily do so.

For the purpose of a quorum, a corporation which is itself a member of a company and which has authorised some person to act as its representative at any meeting of the company, under the provisions of s 375 of the Act, is regarded as personally present, not as present by proxy if its representative is present.[3] Restrictions imposed upon a proxy do not apply to such a representative. A person present by his or her attorney is not present in person, nor, it seems, is an executor of a deceased member counted for the purpose of a quorum if the article requires the members to be personally present,[4] even if the executor is entitled to be on the register though not yet entered.

(2) One-person meetings

The general principle that one person cannot constitute the quorum at a general meeting has already been noted. Some exceptions to this principle are, however, recognised. The obvious exception is for companies incorporated as, or which become, single member companies under s 1(3A) for which there is a statutory exception under s 370A. Similarly, in relation to class shares, it was held in *East v Bennett Bros*,[5] that the assent of the only preference shareholder was equivalent to a resolution passed by a separate meeting of preference shareholders.

In the case of general meetings, there are, moreover, two statutory exceptions to the rule that one person cannot constitute a meeting. The first relates to the Secretary of State's power under s 367 to call a meeting where there has been default in complying with s 366 on the calling of annual general meetings. Section 367(2) provides that, in giving directions for the calling of such a meeting, the Secretary of State may direct that one member of the company present in person or by proxy 'shall be deemed to constitute a meeting'. The second relevant statutory provision

---

3   *In re Kelantan Cocoa Nut Estates Ltd* [1920] WN 274.
4   *Re Bowling & Welby's Contract* [1895] 1 Ch 663.
5   [1911] 1 Ch 163.

is s 371, which deals with the power of the court to order a meeting. Again, s 371(2) allows the court to direct that one member present in person or by proxy is 'deemed to constitute a meeting'. The fact that both s 367(2) and s 371(2) use the expression 'deemed' suggests statutory recognition of the fact that one person could not ordinarily constitute a meeting and, therefore, reinforces the general rule about one-person meetings of the members.

(3) Special class quorums

In the case of class meetings held to resolve a proposed variation of class rights, s 125 (6) requires a quorum of two persons holding or representing by proxy at least one-third in nominal value of the issued shares of the class in question. So high a quorum is not always easy to assemble, and if no quorum is obtained the meeting will be adjourned. The subsection provides that at an adjourned meeting the quorum is one person, either in person or by proxy, holding shares of the class in question.

(4) Abuse of quorum provisions

Where a member refuses to attend a meeting and thus prevents the formation of a quorum, this will be a ground for the court ordering the holding of a meeting under s 371.[6] Presumably, the same consequence would follow in a situation where the articles require that the meeting remains quorate throughout, as in Table A, reg 40, and members persistently frustrate the transaction of business by leaving the meeting.

CHAIRMAN

(1) Appointment

In the absence of any provisions in the articles as to who is to be chairman of a general meeting, any member elected by the members present may be a chairman (s 370(5)). However, the articles generally provide who is to take the chair at general meetings. Regulation 42 of Table A, for example, provides for the chairman of the board of directors or, in the absence of that chairman, some other director nominated by the directors, to be the chairman of a general meeting. If neither of these are present within 15 minutes of the time fixed for holding the meeting, or if neither is willing to act, the directors are to elect one of themselves to be chairman of the meeting and if there is only one director present and willing to act, that director shall be the chairman. These rules apply even if the chairman of

---

6   *Re El Sombrero Ltd* [1958] Ch 900; *Re H & R Paul & Son Ltd* (1974) 118 SJ 166; *Re Opera Photographic Ltd* [1989] BCLC 763.

the board of directors, or some other director appointed to chair the general meeting, is not him- or herself a member of the company. Regulation 43 provides that if no director is willing, or none is present within 15 minutes, the members present may choose one of themselves to be the chairman.[7]

(2) Authority

The authority which a chairman has is usually delegated to him or her by the company under its articles or by that meeting by which he or she is appointed. Where a number of persons assemble and put a person in the chair they confer on that person by agreement the conduct of that assembled body. The person presiding over a general meeting of members is, in the capacity as chairman of the meeting, acting as the representative of the members present at the meeting, not as the representative of the directors. The chairman's authority, which is acquired from the meeting, enables the chairman to do everything required to ascertain the opinion of the majority, to allow a proper discussion of the questions to be decided, and to ensure that the proceedings are conducted in accordance with the articles. The chairman must, of course, act fairly and allow all members who wish to speak to a motion to have a reasonable opportunity to do so, even if there is clearly a majority who have already made up their minds.

(3) Duties

It is the duty of the chairman to preserve order; to conduct the proceedings in a proper manner; and to take care that the sense of the meeting is properly ascertained with regard to any question which is properly before the meeting.[8] Thus, in the absence of express provisions in the articles, 'the details of the proceedings must be regulated by the persons present and by the chairman, and if his decision is quarrelled with it must be regulated by the majority of those present'.[9] But where the articles expressly provide for the conduct of meetings, the provisions contained therein must be followed.

(4) Powers

The powers of the chairman must be exercised impartially. It is the chairman's duty to conduct the meeting in such a way that the business thereof is facilitated and the results of that business clearly defined. It is the duty of a chairman to maintain his or her ruling on points of procedure. If the chairman's ruling is wrong, he or she may, of course, be called upon to answer for his or her conduct, and legal proceedings may follow, which may result in the proceedings of the meeting being

---

7   *Re Salcombe Hotel Development Corporation Ltd* [1991] BCLC 44. See also *Re Bradford Investments* [1991] BCLC 224, in which a proxy assumed the position of temporary chairman in order to elect a proper chairman.
8   *National Dwelling Society v Sykes* [1894] 3 Ch 159; *R v D'Oyly* (1840) 12 A&E 139.
9   *Wandsworth Gaslight Co v Wright* (1870) 22 LT 404.

declared invalid.[10] Generally, however, the chairman of a general meeting has prima facie to decide all incidental questions which arise at such a meeting and require decision at that time.[11]

This general power of the chairman and its concomitant limitations have been summarised as follows:

> 'Where a chairman frustrates the business of a meeting by wilfully and without good reason preventing that business from being considered, the meeting may in view of his gross violation of duty supersede him as chairman and go on to transact the business. But if in good faith the chairman gives a decision upon a matter of difficulty, such as has arisen in connection with the notice in this case, I am not prepared to hold that his decision can be ignored and overturned there and then. In my opinion in such a case his decision must stand until it is set aside by the Court, or by a general meeting properly convened for that purpose.[12]

More specifically, the chairman has the following powers.

(a) To regulate the course of the proceedings at the meeting
In the case of dispute the chairman is entitled to determine who should address the meeting, and protect the speaker from interruption. The chairman is also entitled to prevent discussion taking place which is not relevant to the business of the meeting. This aspect of the chairman's role is discussed further in Chapter 8.

The business transacted must come within the scope of the notice given, and the chairman should refuse to allow any proposed resolution to be put to the meeting which does not come within the scope of the notice. The chairman is bound, however, to allow the proposal of all legitimate and germane resolutions and amendments, and a refusal to do so will invalidate that part of the proceedings, because such refusal may amount to the withdrawal of a material and relevant question from the meeting. In *Henderson v Bank of Australasia*, Cotton LJ observed: 'the chairman was entirely wrong in refusing to put the amendment, and . . . the resolutions which were passed cannot be allowed to stand, because the chairman, under a mistaken idea as to what the law was which ought to have regulated his conduct, prevented a material question from being brought before the meeting'.[13]

Amendments to resolutions must also come within the scope of the notice convening the meeting and conform to any provisions of the articles as to notice or other requirements. Much difficulty may arise from amendments. It seems to be the case that no amendment of any substance should be accepted to a special or extraordinary resolution (see Chapter 3). So far as an ordinary resolution is

---

10 *Henderson v Bank of Australasia* (1890) 45 ChD 330.
11 *Re Indian Zoedone Co* (1884) 26 ChD 70.
12 These words are believed to have been used by Lord Wark in *Melville v Graham-Yooll*, an unreported case referred to in [1936] SLT 54.
13 (1890) 45 ChD 330, 346.

concerned, notice of an amendment is not necessary, at any rate so long as the amendment cuts down the effect of the resolution, notice of which was originally given, or if the notice stated that the resolution might be passed with such alterations as should be agreed upon.[14] No amendment radically altering the originally proposed resolution should be accepted. If there is the slightest doubt as to whether an amendment is in order or not, it should be allowed to be put. This will safeguard the ultimate resolution if it turns out in the end that the amendment is in fact relevant and germane to the resolution. The chairman often has to make up his or her mind at once upon the validity of amendments, and when the chairman is fairly certain that the amendment will be lost, there is no real harm done in allowing an amendment which may not be covered by the notice of the meeting. Thus, a chairman should not reject an amendment, if proposed, on the grounds that it has no chance of success. To do so would put the original resolution in danger of a technical objection, which may have no substance in fact.

Where the chairman does rule an amendment out of order, there is no obligation on the part of the mover of the amendment to contest that ruling or to leave the meeting. It is not necessary for the mover to keep up an altercation with the chairman, nor does the mover lose any right to later object by acting under the ruling of the chairman.[15]

Where notice has been given of several resolutions, each resolution must, if any member so requires, be put separately and not en bloc. The poll thereon must in any event be taken separately.[16] In this context, it should also be noted that at a meeting of a public company a motion for the appointment of two or more directors cannot be made by a single resolution unless that course is resolved upon by the meeting without dissent. If it is not so resolved, the appointment of each director must be resolved upon by a separate resolution (s 292).

(b) To close the meeting with its consent
When the views of the minority have been heard, it is competent for the chairman, with the sanction of a vote of the meeting, to declare the discussion closed and to put the question to vote.[17] This procedure can be important if a minority are wasting time and repeating arguments or digressing into irrelevancies.

(c) To adjourn the meeting
See Chapter 10.

---

14 *Betts & Co v MacNaghten* [1910] 1 Ch 430.
15 *Henderson v Bank of Australasia* (1890) 45 ChD 330.
16 *Blair Open Hearth Furnace Co v Reigart* (1913) 108 LT 665.
17 *Wall v London & Northern Assets Corporation* [1898] 2 Ch 469.

(d) To make arrangements for taking a poll and to receive or reject proxies

The chairman's decision as to the rejection of proxies will be decisive until reversed by the court.

(e) To give a casting vote

The chairman has no casting vote unless it is so provided in the articles. Table A, reg 50 does so provide. A casting vote may be exercised only if there is an equality of valid votes. If the chairman does not exercise his or her casting vote in such a situation, the motion is not carried. A chairman may also have an ordinary vote if he or she is a member of the company (as is usually the case). A chairman may give a contingent or hypothetical vote to come into operation if, in the course of subsequent proceedings, it should appear that there has been an equality of valid votes.[18]

Since a casting vote is conferred on the office of chairman, and not on the individual, it must be exercised as a fiduciary power in what the chairman considers to be the interest of the company as a whole.

(f) To declare the result of voting

Section 378(4) provides that, unless a poll is demanded, the chairman's declaration that an extraordinary or special resolution is carried is conclusive without proof of the number or proportion of the votes recorded for or against the resolution. Regulation 47 of Table A extends this principle to the voting on all resolutions by providing that, unless a poll is demanded, a declaration by the chairman that a resolution has been carried, carried unanimously, carried by a particular majority, lost, or lost by a particular majority and an entry made in the minutes to that effect is conclusive without proof of the number or proportion of the votes recorded for or against the resolution. A properly made and bona fide chairman's declaration under these provisions will prevent the question being reopened in legal proceedings even if evidence is forthcoming that the chairman's declaration was wrong.[19] The only exceptions to this are: first, where there is an apparent error, such as where the chairman states the number of votes given and they are insufficient[20] or where it is plain on the face of the proceedings that the requisite majority was not obtained;[21] secondly, where there is no apparent opposition to a proposal, but the chairman omits to put it to a show of hands, as required by Table A, reg 46.[22]

Under reg 58 of Table A the chairman has the final and conclusive power to decide on the qualification of any person to vote at a company meeting. In the absence of

---

18   *Bland v Buchanan* [1901] 2 KB 75.
19   *Arnot v United African Lands* [1901] 1 Ch 518.
20   *Re Caratal (New) Mines* [1902] 2 Ch 498.
21   *Re Clark & Co* [1911] SC 243.
22   *Re Citizens Theatre Ltd* [1946] SC 14.

bad faith or fraud, the court will not interfere with the exercise by the chairman of this power.[23]

Finally, it should be noted by way of a proviso to the foregoing that no decision of the chairman will be conclusive if it relates to a resolution that was not in accordance with the notice for the meeting. In *Betts & Co v MacNaghten*,[24] it was held that notwithstanding a declaration by the chairman, the notice of the meeting is part of the proceedings and may be looked at to see if the resolution is in accordance with it. If it is not, the chairman's declaration that the resolution was passed is not conclusive. Neither is a chairman's declaration conclusive where there is no quorum, since there would be no properly constituted meeting.

---

23   *Wall v London & Northern Assets Corporation (No 2)* [1899] 1 Ch 550; *Wall v Exchange Investment Corporation* [1926] Ch 143.
24   [1910] 1 Ch 430.

Chapter 7

BUSINESS OF MEMBERS' MEETINGS

INTRODUCTION

The articles may provide that all business conducted at extraordinary general meetings, and all except certain specified matters to be conducted at annual general meetings, is to be special business; and the articles may further provide that notice of a general meeting is, in the case of special business, to specify the general nature of that business. Such provisions were found in regs 50 and 52 of Table A to the 1948 legislation. The business specified in reg 52 as not being special business of an annual general meeting consisted of the consideration of the accounts, balance sheets and reports of the directors and auditors, the election of directors in place of those retiring, and the appointment of, and the fixing of the remuneration of, the auditors. The result of an article such as this is to make it unnecessary to specify these matters, because they are not special business, in the notice convening the meeting. In the present Table A, however, there is no equivalent provision to reg 52. Accordingly, where the articles are in the form of the present Table A, all business to be transacted at an annual general meeting is, it appears, special business and must be specified in the notice.

READING THE NOTICE

Meetings are sometimes opened by the secretary reading the notice convening the meeting, or the chairman asking the meeting to agree that the notice be taken as read. Even the latter is a somewhat pompous formality, and quite unnecessary. There is no statutory requirement to read the notice. It is far more sensible for the chairman or proposer of each resolution to read the proposed resolution when its turn comes, so that shareholders are aware at the relevant time of what they are considering. Sometimes the minutes of the previous meeting are then read and formally verified as correct, but, unless required by the articles, this proceeding at a general meeting is unnecessary and, generally, a waste of time.

CONSIDERATION OF ACCOUNTS ETC

A private company may pass an elective resolution under s 252 to dispense with the laying of accounts and reports before the general meeting. In all other cases, s 241 requires the directors to lay before the general meeting (in practical terms, the annual general meeting) a copy of the profit and loss accounts and a balance sheet for each financial year. They may also be required to lay a copy of the group accounts (see s 227) before the meeting. This must be done within seven months (for public companies) or 10 months (for private companies) after the end of the 'relevant accounting reference period' (s 244(1)), which is effectively the end of the financial year (s 244(6)).[1] In addition, the directors' report must be laid before the general meeting with the accounts (s 241). The auditors' report should also be laid with the accounts unless the company is exempt from the provisions of the Companies Acts relating to the audit of accounts in a particular year under s 249A – it is an 'audit exempt' company. See Appendix for a precedent. The requirements for the auditor's report are laid down in ss 235 and 236. In particular, it should be noted that under s 235(3) the auditors are required, if they consider that the information given in the directors' report for the relevant financial year is not consistent with the annual accounts for that year, to state that fact in their report. The requirements for the directors' report are found in ss 234 and 234A. These sections require, among other things, that the directors' report should contain a fair review of the development of the company's business and that of its subsidiaries during the financial year and state the amount (if any) recommended to be paid by way of dividend and the amount (if any) proposed to be carried to reserve (s 234(1)). There are, however, a number of other requirements for the directors' report contained in these sections and in Sch 7 to the Act. Failure to comply with all of these provisions is an offence (s 243(5)).

Under s 238(1), copies of the annual accounts together with copies of the directors' report and, unless the company is audit exempt, the auditor's report must be sent to every member of the company, every debenture holder of the company and to all other persons entitled to receive notices of general meetings of the company, for example the auditors, at least 21 days before the date of the meeting at which the documents are to be laid. They need not be sent to members or debenture holders who are not entitled to receive notices of meetings if the company does not know the addresses of such people; and if joint holders of shares and debentures are not all entitled to notices of meetings, copies need only be sent to those joint holders who are entitled to notices or, if none is entitled, to one such joint holder (s 238(2)). In the case of companies not having a share capital, these documents need not be sent to members or debenture holders who are not entitled to receive notices of meetings of the company (s 238(3)). All members may agree to copies being sent

---

1	As to the calculation of the company's financial year end and the 'accounting reference period', see ss 243 and 244 of the Companies Act 1985.

outside the time-limit of 21 days (s 238(4)), but in the absence of such agreement the company and every officer in default commits an offence if there is failure to comply with the time-limit (s 238(5)).

The chairman usually begins by making some comments on the accounts, then he or she may explain the position of the company, giving such further information concerning its affairs as he or she thinks may properly be made known, and, finally, conclude by moving that the reports and accounts be adopted. This is usually seconded by another director with a few remarks, following which the members present at the meeting are free to comment on or criticise the reports, accounts and the chairman's speech. So far as it is possible without prejudice to the interests of the company, the directors should answer freely all inquiries regarding the accounts and the company's affairs. However, they are not bound to answer in general meeting any questions which they consider undesirable, in the best interests of the company, to answer.

Unless steps have been taken in advance by dissatisfied members, there is usually very little that the members can do at an annual general meeting if they are dissatisfied with the directors' report or the conduct of the directors. They can vote against the resolution for the adoption of the report, but even if the resolution is lost, this has no effect other than to indicate the disapproval of a majority at the meeting. If the resolution is lost, an attempt is sometimes made by the dissatisfied members to appoint a committee of inspection from among their number to look into the affairs of the company, but this cannot be done without proper notice of a resolution to this effect having been given. This procedure is, in any case, valueless, since the resolution does not give the committee any powers of investigation for requiring information. So long as the directors remain as the directors of the company, they retain their powers as such and the company cannot remove the control of its affairs from them.[2] In some cases, where the meeting proves hostile, the directors may agree to give certain information to a committee appointed by the dissatisfied members and to adjourn the meeting until that has been done. They are not, however, bound to do so.

Dissatisfied shareholders may also make an application to the Secretary of State to investigate a company under s 431, but only if they together number 200 shareholders or 10 per cent of the holders of the issued shares, or, where the company has no share capital, one-fifth of the persons on the register of members (s 431(2)). The applicants for such an investigation must give supporting evidence showing they have good reason for requiring an investigation (s 431(3)) and they may also be required to give security (s 431(4)). Even after all this has been done, there is no guarantee that an investigation will be ordered. The unpredictability of the outcome of applications for company investigations means that where the majority of members of a company disapprove of the conduct of the directors they

---

2   *Automatic Self-Cleansing Filter Co v Cunninghame* [1906] 2 Ch 34.

are probably better off availing themselves of the power conferred by s 303 to remove the directors by ordinary resolutions and appoint others in their place by like resolutions (see Chapter 3). This, however, can only be done if the requisite notices have been given, and if the notices have not been given in time for an annual general meeting, a subsequent meeting will have to be requisitioned for this purpose.

DECLARING A DIVIDEND

Assuming the report is adopted, one of the directors usually then moves the payment of the dividend recommended therein. Articles usually provide that the company in general meeting may declare dividends, but that no dividend shall exceed the amount recommended by the directors, see, for example, Table A, reg 102.

ELECTION OF DIRECTORS

The articles generally contain provisions relating to the retirement and election of directors. For example, Table A provides that at the first annual general meeting all the directors shall retire from office and at subsequent annual general meetings one-third of the directors (being those who have been longest in office) shall retire (regs 73 and 74). This requirement that directors 'retire by rotation' is often disapplied in the articles of private companies. For companies to which these provisions do apply, Table A goes on to provide that, at the meeting at which a director retires under the rotation provisions, if the company does not fill the vacated office, the retiring director if willing to act is deemed reappointed. The exceptions are if it is resolved not to fill the office or a resolution for the retiring director's re-election is lost.[3] Generally, the intention to propose any person (other than a retiring director or a person recommended by the directors) for election to the board at any general meeting must, under reg 76, be given to the company with notice of the willingness to act of the person proposed to be elected. Regulation 76(a) provides that such notice must be given not less than 14 or more than 35 clear days before the meeting. Where the directors propose to recommend someone other than a retiring director for election to the position of director then, under reg 77, they must give notice of that fact to the company not less than seven or more than 28 clear days before the meeting. Subject to all these provisions, appointments under Table A to the office of director may be made by ordinary resolution (reg 78) and, for the period between annual general meetings, the board may (subject to certain provisos) appoint someone to be a director (reg 79).

---

3   See *Grundt v Great Boulder Proprietary Gold Mines Ltd* [1948] Ch 145.

In the case of a public company, the appointment of each director must, to be valid, be effected by a separate resolution unless the meeting agrees without a dissentient to a motion for the appointment of two or more directors being made by a single resolution (s 292(1)). A resolution moved in contravention of that section is void and the persons thereby intended to be appointed directors will not be so appointed (s 292(2)). The section also provides that if an election is thereby avoided and the office of a retiring director is in consequence not filled, no provision for the retiring director's automatic reappointment such as in reg 75 of Table A referred to above is to apply (s 292(2)).

THE POSITION OF AUDITOR

The Eighth EC Company Law Directive made provision with respect to the eligibility of a person to become a company auditor. The requirements of the Directive in this respect are implemented by Part II of the Companies Act 1989. Under these provisions, either an individual or a firm may be appointed as a company auditor (s 25(2)), provided, of course, that they comply with the other requirements as to eligibility, including the requirement of sufficient independence in s 27. Bodies corporate may also be appointed as auditors, subject to compliance with similar eligibility requirements. The provisions on appointment, removal and resignation of auditors are found in Part XI, Chapter V of the Companies Act 1985. Under these provisions, only dormant and audit exempt companies are exempt from the obligation to appoint auditors (ss 249A, 384(1) and 388A). However, a private company may resolve by elective resolution to dispense with the annual appointment of auditors (s 386). It should also be noted that where a private company has passed an elective resolution under s 252 to dispense with the laying of accounts and reports before the general meeting, then s 385A modifies its obligations in relation to the appointment of auditors.

Except in the case of a company which has elected to dispense with the laying of accounts, a new company's first auditor may be appointed by the directors to hold office until the end of the first general meeting before which the accounts are laid (s 385(3)). In the case of a company which has elected to dispense with the laying of accounts, the first auditor may be appointed by the directors either:

(i)   before the period of 28 days beginning with the day on which copies of the first annual accounts are sent to members under s 238 and until the end of that period, or

(ii) where a notice has been given under s 253(2) requiring the laying of the accounts before the company in general meeting, at any time before that meeting until the beginning of the meeting (s 385A(3)).

If the directors fail to appoint an auditor under these provisions, the company in general meeting may do so (ss 385(4) and 385A(4)). Thereafter, every company must appoint auditors at each general meeting before which the accounts are laid (s 385(2)), to hold office from the end of that meeting until the end of the next such meeting.

This obviously does not apply, however, to:

(i)   audit exempt companies;
(ii)   dormant companies;
(iii) companies which have elected to dispense with annual appointment under s 386;
(iv)   companies which have elected to dispense with the laying of accounts.

In the latter case, auditors must be appointed before the end of the period of 28 days, which commences with the day on which the accounts are sent to the members. The appointment so made runs from the end of that 28-day period until the next time for appointing auditors, or where notice has been given requiring the laying of accounts before the company in general meeting, before the conclusion of the general meeting to hold office from the conclusion of the general meeting until the next time for appointing auditors (s 385A(2)). If the company fails to make an appointment, it must give notice to the Secretary of State, who may fill the vacancy (s 387). Should a casual vacancy arise, the remaining auditors may continue to act and the directors or the company in general meeting may appoint an auditor to fill the casual vacancy (s 388).

The remuneration of auditors is fixed by the company in general meeting, or in such manner as the company in general meeting may determine (s 390A(1)). Where auditors are appointed by the directors or the Secretary of State, their remuneration may be fixed by the directors or the Secretary of State, respectively (s 390A(2)). (Section 390B governs remuneration of auditors for non-audit work.)

The company has power by ordinary resolution to remove an auditor before the expiry of his or her term of office (s 391); however, such a resolution requires special notice (s 391A). (Special notice is considered in Chapter 3.) Notice that such a resolution has been passed must be given to the Registrar of Companies within 14 days (s 391(2)). The removal is effective even though it may amount to a breach of contract between the company and the auditor, who in that case retains the right to compensation or damages for the termination of his or her appointment or of any other appointment which terminates along with his or her appointment as auditor (s 391(1) and (3)).

The requirement of special notice where the auditor is being removed, either before the expiration of the auditor's term of office, or by virtue of someone else being appointed in place of a retiring auditor (s 391A(1)) is part of a number of requirements designed to bolster the independence of auditors. For the same reason, special notice is also required in order for the company in general meeting to fill a casual vacancy or to reappoint an auditor appointed by the directors to fill a casual vacancy (s 388(3)). In summary, this means that special notice will always be required for resolutions concerning the filling of the position of auditor unless the resolution is merely to reappoint an auditor appointed at the last general meeting or to reappoint the company's first auditors appointed by the directors.

On receiving a resolution requiring special notice in relation to the position of auditor, the company must forthwith send a copy of the resolution to the person it is proposed to appoint or remove (ss 388(4) and 391A(2)). Where it is proposed to appoint someone other than a retiring auditor to the position of auditor or to remove an auditor before the auditor's term of office expires, the retiring auditor or the auditor whose removal is proposed may make written representations concerning the resolution to the company and may request the company to notify its members of those representations (s 391A(3)). The company must then state that representations have been received in any notice of the resolution given to members and must send a copy of the representations to every member to whom notice of the meeting is or has been sent (s 391A(4)), unless the representations are received too late to allow this to be done. If the representations are received too late for inclusion in the notice sent to members or the company fails to comply, the auditor may demand that the representations are read out at the meeting (s 391A(5)). This is subject to the usual proviso that the court may accede to the request of the company or an aggrieved person that the representations are not sent out or read at the meeting if it is satisfied that the rights are being used to secure needless publicity for defamatory material (s 391A(6)).

An auditor removed in mid-term by an extraordinary general meeting may attend and speak at the general meeting at which his or her term of office would normally have expired and any general meeting at which it is proposed to fill the vacancy caused by his or her removal (ss 391(4) and 390). The auditor must, accordingly, be given all relevant notices of, and other communications relating to, such meetings which any member is entitled to receive.

The right of an auditor whose position has been terminated to attend and speak at certain meetings is, in fact, an extension of the rights enjoyed by all auditors while in office to receive all notices and communications which members are entitled to receive, and to attend and be heard at general meetings (s 390(1)). Similarly, the auditors have the right to receive all communications relating to statutory written resolutions (which are discussed in Chapter 3) as are required to be supplied to a member. (Where an auditor is not appointed annually his or her position may be terminated in accordance with s 393.)

An auditor may resign by depositing written notice of resignation at the company's registered office (s 392(1)). The resignation will be effective only if it states that there are no circumstances connected with the resignation which the auditor considers should be brought to the attention of members or creditors, or if it contains a statement of such circumstances (s 392(1)). The company must send a copy of the notice of resignation to the Registrar of Companies within 14 days (s 392(3)) and, if the notice contains a statement of special circumstances which the auditor considers ought to be brought to the attention of members and creditors, the company must, within the same period, send copies to all members and creditors entitled to receive the accounts under s 238 or must apply to the court on the ground that the statement is being used to secure needless publicity for defamatory material (s 394(3)). If such an application to the court is made, the company must notify the resigning auditor (s 394(4)) and if the resigning auditor does not receive notice of any application within 21 days from the deposit of the statement at the registered office, the resigning auditor must lodge the statement with the Registrar of Companies within a further seven-day period (s 394(5)). Where an application is made to the court by the company and upheld, then the company must send a statement setting out the effect of the court order to everyone entitled to receive accounts, within 14 days of the court order (s 394(6)). Where, on the other hand, the court does not uphold the company's application, then the company must circulate the document as ordinarily required and notify the resigning auditor, who must in turn send a copy of the statement to the Registrar within seven days of receiving notice of the court order (s 394(7)). These provisions are designed to ensure, inter alia, that company members are not left in a state of ignorance about disputes involving matters affecting the company's financial management. Failure on the part of the resigning auditor, the company or any company officer to comply with the requirements concerning circulation of resigning auditors' statements in s 394 is an offence (s 394A).

In addition to the rights under s 394 concerning circulation of statements of resigning auditors to the effect that special circumstances exist, a resigning auditor who has delivered such a statement may give the directors, at the same time, a requisition to call an extraordinary general meeting to receive and consider the resigning auditor's explanation of those circumstances (s 392A(2)). The resigning auditor may also call on the company to circulate to members a written statement of those circumstances before the general meeting at which his or her term of office would otherwise have expired or before any general meeting at which it is proposed to fill the place vacated by the auditor or which he or she has requisitioned (s 392A(3)). The company must then in any notice of the meeting inform members that the statement has been made and, subject to the usual proviso concerning an application to the court in the case of allegedly defamatory matter (s 392A(7)), send a copy to every member to whom notice of the meeting is or has been sent (s 392A(4)) or, if it fails to do this, have the statement read out at the meeting (s 392A(6)). The period of notice for the meeting must not exceed 28 days, and the directors must proceed to convene the meeting within 21 days of deposit of the requisition, failure to do so being a criminal offence (s 392A(5)). The auditor is entitled to attend the relevant meeting, receive notices and documents relating to it, and speak at the meeting on the business concerning the auditor as a former auditor (s 392A(8)).

SPECIAL BUSINESS

This can be transacted at an annual general meeting provided due notice has been given. There is no need to transact special business at an extraordinary general meeting, although this is often done.

Chapter 8

CONDUCT OF MEMBERS' MEETINGS

INTRODUCTION

The conduct of a members' meeting may be governed by statute, the articles, any internal operating procedures and custom. The nature of these various rules will depend upon the character of the company holding the meeting, but they should be clear, explicit, and free from any ambiguity. They should be fair and reasonable, and interpreted in an impartial manner. From them the chairman obtains most of his or her power and they form an invaluable authority to which the chairman can appeal. But the chairman must know the rules and understand their purport and meaning, otherwise it may lead to unnecessary conflict with those entitled to attend the meeting.

Companies' operating procedures (if any) must not be inconsistent with the relevant statutory provisions or the company's articles.

Where there are no operating procedures or they are inadequate, then either the usual customs of the company (if any) or the usual practice of previous meetings may be followed. In a simple case, however, the difficulty may be overcome by the chairman exercising his common sense and bearing in mind that it is his or her duty to ascertain the views of the meeting and act in the best interests of the company.

Rules should safeguard the general rights of those entitled to attend the meeting and should not crush the rights of minorities. When once agreed to, any alteration to operating procedures or custom should be made only after proper notice has been given to the persons affected.

Operating procedures are of great assistance to chairman, members, and officers alike; they prevent misapprehension of the powers of the meeting, avoid confusion and disorder, and facilitate the dispatch and conduct of business.

An attendee at the meeting may dispute the chairman's conduct of the meeting. It is not necessary that he or she should persist in disputing the chairman's decision at a meeting in order to safeguard his or her right to impeach the validity of the ruling after the meeting. If the chairman improperly deprives a person of a right to which he or she is legally entitled, the validity of the proceedings may be impeached afterwards in any event.

The general meeting open to all the members of the company entitled to attend under the articles is generally the ultimate authority for all the business transacted by that company. Unless there is an express or statutory delegation of authority to the directors, a committee or some other body, no reports or resolutions of delegated bodies are binding until they have been confirmed by the members. In most cases, however, the majority of the day-to-day acts and decisions of the company are delegated to the directors (see Chapter 2).

COMMITTEES

'A committee means a person or persons to whom powers are committed which would otherwise by exercised by another body.'[1] A committee may consist of one person but normally consists of several. It exercises limited powers, which may be modified or withdrawn by its appointing authority. The powers of committees should be clearly set forth in their appointment. The chairman and the members of a committee are normally members of the appointing body. In the case of a limited company it is competent for the members of the company to delegate most of their powers (not reserved to them by statute) to the directors in such a way that those powers can no longer be exercised by the members themselves. In such cases, unless the articles provide otherwise, the exercise by the directors of the powers delegated to them cannot be controlled by the company in general meeting, and to enable the company to do this, it would be necessary to alter the articles (see Chapter 2).

In turn, the directors may appoint a committee comprising one or more of their number to deal with some specific branches of their work. A committee of the directors can only act within the limits prescribed by its appointing authority, ie the board. However, unlike the delegation of their powers to the directors by the members, delegation of their powers by directors to a committee of the board does not imply a parting with the powers granted by the board. The board remains responsible for the decisions and acts of its committees. Such powers delegated to the committee can be resumed at any time by the board.[2] A committee of the board must report to the board regularly and fully.

A committee may come into existence and have certain powers even without being expressly appointed. In such a case the powers and jurisdiction of the committee will be implied. An example of such a committee, and the limits on its jurisdiction, is found in the trade union case of *Abbott v Sullivan*.[3]

---

1   *Re Taurine Co* (1883) 25 ChD 132.
2   *Huth v Clarke* (1890) 25 QBD 391.
3   [1952] 1 KB 189.

DISCUSSION AND DEBATE

Under common law the conduct and control of the discussion or debate is mainly in the hands of the chairman, who should be impartial in its management. The following practices are, in the absence of specific regulation by the Act, articles or operating procedures, it is suggested, appropriate:

(1) Every member who so desires should, where practicable, have an opportunity of speaking upon each resolution; no second speech should be allowed except that the mover of the resolution should have a right of reply. Every speech should be addressed to the chairman in his or her capacity as chairman. Every member who speaks should direct their speech strictly to the resolution under discussion, or to an explanation, or to a question of order. Sometimes a time-limit on the length of speeches is fixed, which may be varied with the consent of the meeting.

(2) The order in which members should speak is determined by the chairman, who should endeavour to ascertain either the implied or express wishes of the meeting on this matter, any conflict of opinion being settled by vote of the meeting. According to custom, the member who is entitled to address the meeting is the one who first rises to speak or otherwise indicates a desire to speak and who is observed by the chairman. If a meeting declines to accept the choice of the chairman as to who shall speak, for example, when several members simultaneously indicate a desire to address the meeting, it is open to the meeting to resolve this matter by formal motion (for example, that Mrs A be now heard). However, deference to the chairman is a principle which should be observed. Furthermore, it is not open to the majority to prevent the views of the minority being put forward.[4]

(3) The chairman should impartially allow supporters and opponents of the resolution equal opportunities of speaking, and have regard to the rights of minorities.

(4) The chairman should insist on members refraining from unseemly interruptions or making a running commentary on the remarks of the speaker. Similarly the holding of private conversations sotto voce during the debate, or any other conduct tending to disturb the meeting should be prevented by the chairman. The chairman should call a member to order for repetition, unbecoming language, or any other breach of order, and may direct such member, if speaking, to discontinue his or her speech.

(5) Points of order which may be raised by any member, whether the member has previously spoken or not, should be taken as soon as they are brought to the notice of the chairman. Explanations, which should be brief and to the point, must not introduce new topics. The chairman should not allow a speech or

---

4   *Constable v Harris* (1824) T&R 496; *Wall v London and Northern Assets Corporation* [1898] 2 Ch 480.

debate to follow an explanation. The chairman's decision on points of order is final.

(6)   Discussion must be relevant to the subject under debate. Members who ignore this rule, or who use offensive language, or impute improper motives to colleagues, should be cautioned by the chairman, and, in the event of persistent disregard of the authority of the chair, should be requested to retire from the meeting, and, if necessary, be removed from the meeting.

These rules are appropriate for private meetings of members entitled to attend and participate. Broadly similar principles should, it is thought, be applied to company meetings such as general meetings of the members on premises to which admission is controlled by the organisers of the meeting. But at such a meeting the chairman's position, although no more and no less important, is probably stronger. Since (unless granted by the terms of admission) there is no entitlement for those admitted to the meeting to speak, the chairman will have complete discretion in deciding who may address the meeting. The chairman, in such circumstances, has no absolute duty to ensure that everyone who desires to speak is given an adequate chance to do so. However, if the chairman uses his or her discretion arbitrarily, the purpose of the meeting may be undermined.

Chapter 9

VOTING AT MEMBERS' MEETINGS

GENERAL PRINCIPLES

Voting at general meetings of the members generally takes place either on a show of hands or on a poll. The articles of association usually set out the voting rights attached to the shares. Insofar as they do not, s 370(6) applies and gives members, in the case of a company originally having a share capital, one vote for each share or £10 of stock, and in any other case one vote for every member. Although the Act is not specific on this point, s 370(6) presumably applies only to a vote on a poll.[1]

It is common for the articles to deal with these matters and reg 54 of Table A, for example, provides that, subject to any other rights or restrictions attached to the shares, on a show of hands every member present in person and holding shares entitled to vote at the meeting shall have one vote, and on a poll every such member shall have one vote for each share of which that member is the holder. Articles in this form are also consistent with s 372(2)(c) which provides that, subject to the articles, a proxy has a vote only on a poll. Even if, however, the articles provide that a member present by proxy may vote on a show of hands the proxy will only have one vote on the show of hands whether a member of the company or not.[2]

Under case-law, it is clear that the right of an alien enemy to vote personally or by proxy in respect of shares in an English company is suspended during war.[3] At a more quotidian level, articles frequently provide that certain classes of shares, for example preference shares, shall confer no vote at general meetings or shall confer a right to vote at such meetings only on certain specified matters or when the preference dividend is in arrears for a certain period. Most forms of articles also contain a restriction on the right of a member to vote unless all calls or other sums presently payable by the member in respect of shares in the company have been paid (for example Table A, reg 57).

It used to be common to find provisions in articles stating that a member was not entitled to exercise votes in respect of shares until that member had held them for a specified period. In other cases, voting rights were exercisable by a member only

---

1   *Ernest v Loma Gold Mines* [1897] 1 Ch 1.
2   Ibid.
3   *Robson v Premier Oil & Co* [1915] 2 Ch 124.

upon a limited number of shares; thus, if the member held more than that number, he or she had no (or reduced) voting rights in respect of the excess. Neither of these restrictions is common today, but they are still found on occasions.

As between the company and a member, a member may vote as that member pleases (provided the member has not been disqualified by the articles or the Act). Even if the company is aware that the member is, or may be, under an obligation to a third person (including another member) to vote in a certain way or as that other person directs, the company is not entitled to question or reject a vote cast by a member in accordance with the articles.[4] This does not mean, however, that the court, if applied to, would not restrain the exercise of such a vote on behalf of some party other than the company. There are two general classes of cases in which the court will constrain a shareholder to exercise his or her vote in a way dictated by another person. The first class involves certain circumstances in which a member holds shares in which another person has an interest. For example, in the absence of a contract a person in whose name shares are registered, such as a mortgagee, may vote as that person pleases, but where the mortgagee of shares agrees for valuable consideration to vote at general meetings of the company in accordance with the wishes of the mortgagor, the court will enforce the agreement by mandatory injunction.[5] Similarly, an agreement made by a shareholder who has sold his or her shares, to vote in a particular way until the share transfer is registered, is valid and can be enforced,[6] and a member who holds shares as nominee or bare trustee for another is bound to vote as the beneficial owner directs.[7] On the other hand, in the absence of express provisions to the contrary, an unpaid or partly paid vendor of shares, remaining registered in respect of them, retains the right to decide how those shares should be voted.[8] The other class of cases (of considerable commercial importance) in which a shareholder's right to exercise his or her vote will be constrained by an obligation to a specified third party is where that shareholder has entered into a voting agreement with other shareholders to vote in a certain way on a certain issue.[9] However, the company may not be a party to such a contract.[10]

Subject to these types of contractual and equitable restrictions in favour of other specified persons, members may use their vote as they please. They are not subject to a fiduciary duty and motive is immaterial. 'There is no obligation on a shareholder of a company to give his vote merely with a view to what other persons may consider the interests of the company at large. He has a right, if he thinks fit, to give his vote from motives or promptings of what he considers his own individual

4   *Siemens Bros v Burns* [1918] 2 Ch 324.
5   *Puddephatt v Leith, No 1* [1916] 1 Ch 200.
6   *Greenwell v Porter* [1902] 1 Ch 530.
7   *Wise v Lansdell* [1921] 1 Ch 420.
8   *Musselwhite v CH Musselwhite* [1962] Ch 965.
9   *Russell v Northern Bank Development Corporation Ltd* [1992] 1 WLR 589.
10   Ibid.

interest.'[11] This rule is itself, however, subject to the qualification that a majority of the members will not be allowed by the exercise of their votes to commit a fraud on the minority.[12] This means, in effect, that a member must not vote so as to give that member, or that member and others, something which belongs to or ought to belong to the company.[13] Nor may a member vote in a way which benefits that member, or that member and others in their capacity as members, in a way which is detrimental to the interests of other members[14] or which differentiates them, unless, of course, the other members all agree. This qualification on the general rule becomes of greater significance in the case of meetings of a class of members. 'While usually a holder of shares or debentures may vote as his interests direct, he is subject to the further principle that where his vote is conferred on him as a member of a class he must conform to the interest of the class itself when seeking to exercise the power conferred on him in his capacity of being a member.'[15] One of the most important applications of this qualification is found when members of one class are also members of another class. Such members may not exercise votes at one class meeting to benefit themselves as members, perhaps to a greater extent, of the other class. In all these cases the court will not interfere to restrain or set aside votes unless it is clear that the member was exercising the votes improperly. If there has been full explanation of the proposal, and it is supported by members with no different interests, the courts will be slow to conclude that the votes of members who had other interests were not validly cast.

Articles normally contain restrictions on the power of directors to vote at board meetings on contracts or arrangements in which they are interested.[16] No such restrictions apply to them when they vote in their capacity as members at general meetings.[17]

Articles also usually contain regulations for voting by joint holders of shares, and in cases of members of unsound mind (regs 55 and 56 of Table A are examples). Further, articles frequently provide that no objection may be raised to a voter except at a meeting at which the voter tenders a vote, and the articles make the chairman of the meeting the person who decides upon any such objection (see, for example, reg 58). This is an awkward and in one respect possibly a misleading provision. It is awkward because very often other members who might well wish to object may be unaware that a particular person has voted, or may not then know of a conflicting interest which that person has. It is misleading in the sense that if a

---

11 *Pender v Lushington* (1877) 6 ChD 75. For an extreme application of this principle, see *Northern Counties Securities v Jackson and Steeple Ltd* [1974] 1 WLR 1113.
12 *Menier v Hooper's Telegraph Co* (1874) LR 9 Ch 350.
13 For examples see *Menier v Hooper's Telegraph Co*, above, *Cook v Deeks* [1916] 1 AC 554.
14 *Clemens v Clemens Bros Ltd* [1976] 2 All ER 268.
15 *British America Nickel Corporation v O'Brien* [1927] AC at 373; *Goodfellow v Nelson Line* [1912] 2 Ch 324; *Re Holders Investment Trust Ltd* [1971] 1 WLR 583.
16 See regs 85 and 86 of Table A and s 317 of the Companies Act 1985.
17 *East Pant-Du United Mining Co v Merryweather* (1864) 2 H&M 254.

member has voted for improper reasons the court will interfere, if asked, despite
the wording of the article. On the other hand, such an article does seem to mean that
objections to the *qualification* of a voter must be taken at the meeting – where they
may be answered – and not later. Every vote not disallowed is valid and the
chairman's decision is conclusive whether or not his or her mind was directed to
the point by an objection.[18]

SHOW OF HANDS

Unless the articles otherwise provide, voting will in the first instance normally be
by show of hands. As stated above, usually every member personally present and
entitled to vote has one vote only on a show of hands, independent of the number of
shares or proxies that person holds. At a meeting of the members of a company, the
articles of which allow voting by proxy, the chairman, in ascertaining the number
of votes given on a show of hands, must count the vote of each member who holds
proxies as a single vote, and not count a vote for each of the members whose
proxies are held by that person.[19] The vote of a non-member, that is a person not
entitled to vote on his or her own account but who is a proxy for a member, will not,
unless the articles so provide, be counted on a show of hands (s 372(2)(c)).
Regulation 54 of Table A does not so provide. A representative of a corporation,
however, would be entitled to vote on a show of hands by virtue of s 375(2).
Regulation 54 also envisages the vote on a show of hands by a duly authorised
representative of a corporation. Due to the restrictions on non-members voting on a
show of hands, it is desirable that if non-members are admitted to the meeting they
should be known to the chairman to prevent them taking part in such a vote.
Similarly, if members not entitled to vote are entitled to attend, the presence of
such members should be brought to the attention of the chairman.

Regulation 46 of Table A provides that at any general meeting a resolution put to
the vote of the meeting shall be decided on a show of hands, unless a poll is (before
or on the declaration of the result of the show of hands) validly demanded and most
articles contain a similar provision. In such a case, it is not necessary to go through
the procedure of a show of hands. The chairman, or the appropriate number of
members, may demand a poll as soon as the resolution is put, or may demand it
beforehand. However, the virtue of a show of hands, particularly where there is a
bitter proxy battle, is that it enables those who have taken the trouble to attend in
person to express their feelings, even though these may have no effect on the result
of the motion. Regulation 47 of Table A makes the chairman's declaration on a
show of hands conclusive.

---

18   *Marx v Estates & General Investments Ltd* [1975] STC 671.
19   *Ernest v Loma Gold Mines Co* [1897] 1 Ch 1.

DEMANDING A POLL

The articles may contain provisions governing the way in which a poll must be demanded at any general meeting, but all such provisions will be subject to the provisions of s 373 which is overriding. The effect of this section is that:

(a)   articles cannot exclude the right to demand a poll (except on the election of the chairman of a meeting or on the adjournment of a meeting); and
(b)   articles cannot make a demand ineffective if made by
    (i)   at least five members entitled to vote, or
    (ii)   members holding 10 per cent or more of the voting rights of all the members having the right to vote at the meeting, or
    (iii) members holding shares on which 10 per cent or more of the total paid up capital has been paid.

Section 373(2) also provides that a proxy may demand or join in demanding a poll. (See also reg 46 of Table A.)

Modern articles usually provide that the chairman of a meeting may demand a poll, and they sometimes provide that members fewer in number or smaller in holdings than the minimum specified in s 373 may demand a poll. For example, reg 46 of Table A empowers the chairman to demand a poll, and it also permits two members having the right to vote and present in person or by proxy to demand a poll.

If a poll is duly demanded it is the chairman's duty to grant it, and to fix the time and place for the poll in accordance with the articles. This power is a fiduciary power and must be exercised in a reasonable way to enable the members to record their votes. It would not, for example, be reasonable or proper to direct that the poll be taken at midnight on a Saturday, or in a place where members could not conveniently attend.

If the demand is challenged it must, of course, be justified, but it need not be justified if the chairman knows privately that the demand is, in fact, supported by the requisite number.[20] In such a case, it is usually simpler and preferable for the chairman to resolve the point by making the demand. If a poll is not taken after a proper demand for a poll has been made, the resolution which has been challenged is void.[21]

The articles may provide, as does reg 48 of Table A, that the demand for a poll may be withdrawn with the consent of the chairman, in which case any pre-existing vote on a show of hands will remain valid.

---

20   *Re Phoenix Electric Light Co* (1883) 48 LT 260.
21   *R v Cooper* (1870) LR 5 QB 457.

TAKING A POLL

Articles frequently provide that a poll demanded on the election of a chairman or a question of adjournment is to be taken forthwith, but that a poll on any other question is to be taken at such time as the chairman directs, and that business other than that on which the poll is demanded may proceed in the meantime (see, for example, reg 51 of Table A). By reg 49, a poll is to be taken in such manner as the chairman directs (except as provided in reg 51) and the result of the poll is to be deemed to be the resolution of the meeting at which the poll was demanded.

It is, under s 373, competent for articles to provide that no poll may be demanded on the election of a chairman or on a question of adjournment. Accordingly, articles sometimes provide that the election of the chairman or a motion for an adjournment be determined on a show of hands of those members present at the meeting. In such cases, numbers present, and not shares held, are decisive. More usual, however, are articles in the form of reg 51 of Table A providing for any poll to be held immediately on these two questions. For motions on which the articles provide that the chairman shall decide when and how the poll be taken, the chairman's power of decision is a fiduciary one. If the chairman thinks that, in order to obtain the considered views of members, the poll should be fixed for a future date, of which notice can be given, he or she should follow this course. If, on the other hand, the chairman thinks that the matter is too urgent for that course, or that members have already had the opportunity to express their considered views, the chairman should hold the poll as soon as possible.[22] The decision is the chairman's, not the board's. Where the articles provide that a poll shall be taken within seven days of the meeting, at a time and place to be fixed by the directors, such time and place must be fixed after a poll has been demanded and cannot be fixed in advance.[23]

The usual method for taking a poll is to require every member who is entitled to vote to sign a paper (in order to prevent impersonation) headed 'for' or 'against' the motion; the number of votes to which each member is entitled under the articles is inserted against the signature of the member, and these having been added, the chairman declares accordingly.

A member may vote personally at a poll even if he or she was not present when the poll was demanded.[24] If, as is usual, the articles provide that a proxy is effective if deposited a certain number of hours before the taking of a poll, a member who had not previously attended or appointed a proxy may appoint one for this purpose.

---

22   See *Re Chillington Iron Co* (1885) 29 ChD 159.
23   *Re British Flax Producers Company* (1889) 60 LT 215.
24   *Campbell v Maund* (1836) 5 A&E 865.

Resolutions must be put to the poll separately and not en bloc, otherwise the poll is invalid.[25] All the resolutions may, however, be included on one sheet of paper, to be separately marked by the voters.

Scrutineers are often appointed to be present at the counting. Regulation 49 of Table A, for example, provides that the chairman may appoint scrutineers who need not be members. It seems, in any case, that where the articles do not provide for the appointment of scrutineers, they may be appointed by the chairman. Unless the articles require scrutineers, it is not obligatory to have any; but it is advisable for two reasons. First, the presence of independent scrutineers reduces the danger of a poll being subsequently challenged by a dissident member, and secondly, because if, as is usual, the auditors are appointed, they have the staff and experience necessary for conducting the poll. Sometimes where there is a dispute, scrutineers representing the warring parties are appointed jointly, but dissident members have no right to insist on the presence of scrutineers appointed by themselves. There is no duty of confidence on scrutineers or organisers of the poll in relation to the way in which votes are cast, as it is necessary to know how votes are cast in order to determine the validity of the poll.[26]

The right to vote and the number of shares held are determined by reference to the register of the members. 'The register of shareholders, on which there can be no notice of a trust, furnishes the only means of ascertaining whether you have a lawful meeting or a lawful demand for a poll, or of enabling the scrutineers to strike out votes.'[27] Where there is a limitation on the number of votes which any member may exercise, the member may transfer some of his or her shares to trustees on his or her behalf and, if they are duly registered, increase his or her voting power.[28]

The chairman should fix the hours during which the poll is to take place. If the chairman does not do so, he or she cannot close the poll so long as votes are coming in. After waiting a reasonable time, if no more voters present themselves, the chairman may declare the poll closed. The improper exclusion of a voter may invalidate a poll.[29]

Unless the articles specifically provide to the contrary (which Table A does not), a poll cannot be taken by sending voting papers to the members, to be lodged with the company. They or their proxies must attend and give the votes personally.[30]

Section 374 provides that on a poll a member entitled to more than one vote need not use all his or her votes or cast all the votes used in the same way. The object of this provision is to enable a person holding shares as trustee or nominee for more

---

25 *Patent Wood Keg Syndicate Ltd v Pearse* (1906) WN 164.
26 *Haarhaus & Co GmbH v Law Debenture Trust Corp plc* [1988] BCLC 640.
27 *Pender v Lushington* (1877) 6 ChD 70, 78.
28 *Re Stranton Iron and Steel Co* (1873) LR 16 Eq 559.
29 *R v Rector etc of St Mary, Lambeth* (1838) 8 A&E 356.
30 *McMillan v Le Roi Mining Co* [1906] 1 Ch 331.

than one person or being a proxy for more than one member to vote as he or she is instructed, even if different instructions require him or her to vote in different ways.

A poll is regarded as part of the proceedings of the original meeting. 'The taking of a poll is a mere enlargement of the meeting at which it was demanded.'[31] The poll is complete from the day when the result is ascertained and declared, and not from the end of the voting.[32]

PROXIES

The word 'proxy' is used confusingly to describe a person appointed in the place of another to represent him or her, and also the instrument by which such a person is appointed. The right to appoint a proxy is conferred by s 372(1). Under that subsection, a member of a company limited by shares entitled to attend and vote at a meeting is entitled to appoint another person, who need not be a member of the company, as a proxy, to attend and vote instead of the member. With respect to a private company, the subsection also confers on the proxy the same rights to address the meeting as enjoyed by the member appointing the proxy. The subsection does not apply to a company not having a share capital and in that case the right, if any, to appoint a proxy must be conferred by the articles (s 372(2)(a)). The articles of a company limited by guarantee may provide that only existing members may be appointed as proxies – appointment of non-members may be prohibited. Unless otherwise provided by the articles, a proxy may vote only on a poll (s 372(2)(c)). Table A does not otherwise provide and consequently the position arises that a proxy may count towards a quorum under reg 40, but may not vote unless a poll is demanded. As already noted, a proxy has, under s 373(2), the same right to demand or join in demanding a poll as the person who appointed the proxy would have had.

Section 372(2)(b) also provides that a member of a private company is not entitled, unless the articles so provide, to appoint more than one proxy to attend on the same occasion. Regulation 59 in Table A does so provide. In public companies the right is to appoint one or more proxies in any event. This means that a member could in theory appoint one proxy for each share that he or she holds. It does not have the restricted meaning of appointing one person, or failing that person, another, and so on.

The expenses incurred by a board in sending out proxies are properly payable by the company. Indeed the Stock Exchange requires companies whose shares are

---

31   *R v Wimbledon Local Board* (1882) 8 QBD 464; *Shaw v Tati Concessions* [1913] 1 Ch 292.
32   *Holmes v Keyes* [1958] Ch 670. Whether a declaration of the result is strictly necessary is not clear, but it would be difficult, for example, for newly elected directors to act unless they know the result of the vote.

listed to send out proxies for all resolutions to be proposed. In *Peel v London and North Western Railway Co*,[33] it was held that it was the duty of the directors to inform the shareholders of the facts of their policy, and the reason why they considered that this policy should be maintained and supported by the shareholders, and that they were justified in trying to influence and secure votes for this purpose, and accordingly that expenses which had thus been bona fide incurred in the interest of the company were properly payable out of the funds of the company. These expenses included the issuing of stamped proxy papers containing the names of three directors as proposed proxies with a stamped envelope for return. This is an important decision in relation to takeover bids and in cases where a group of shareholders is attacking the directors, for it enables directors to use the company's funds to defend their policy. By virtue of s 372(6), invitations to appoint a person or persons as proxy, if issued at the company's expense, must be sent to all members entitled to vote at the relevant meeting. Failure to observe this rule lays every officer of the company knowingly or wilfully authorising or permitting the default open to a fine. However, a proviso to the subsection makes it clear that no liability will attach to officers who issue to a member, at the member's request, a proxy form or a list of persons willing to act as proxy, provided that the form or list is available to all members entitled to vote.

The Act does not specify any particular form of proxy. Table A offers two types: one where there is an open discretion to the appointee as to how to vote (reg 60); the other where the proxy is directed how to vote (the 'two-way' form) (reg 61). The Stock Exchange requires, for listed companies, the latter form.

Proxy battles have increased in England in recent years, and some of the difficulties which arise could be avoided by a more carefully worded form of proxy. For example, the form should make clear whether the proxy may exercise any discretion on an amendment, or on a motion to adjourn the meeting. These points can be important if, as is usually the case, the proxy appointed is one of the directors, who may represent a large number of shareholders and may be uncertain as to his or her powers. In some cases, the proxy's course of conduct will be easy to decide,[34] but on other occasions the proxy may be unclear as to what he or she can and should do.

The proxy may even find him- or herself in a position where he or she believes that, in the interests of the person by whom the proxy was appointed, the vote should be used in a way different from the direction given in the form of proxy. For example, the proxy may have been directed to vote in favour of a scheme which the directors had recommended, but now finds that a more favourable scheme is offered. In such a case, it seems that the proxy may not vote contrary to his or her authority, but may probably refrain from using the vote altogether, unless under some contractual or

---

33 [1907] 1 Ch 5.
34 See *Re Waxed Papers Ltd* [1937] 2 All ER 481.

fiduciary obligation to the member, for example as the member's solicitor. In that case, the proxy must in principle exercise the vote, as he or she is obliged and not merely authorised. It is sometimes suggested in addition that those who solicit proxies (as directors will frequently do) thereby impose upon themselves such an obligation. This is not clear. It may seem an unduly inflexible control, but if it is otherwise, the protection given to members by the two-way proxy (which in any event is incomplete since the member will usually have heard only the directors' side of the argument) will become largely illusory, as directors would merely exercise those proxies favourable to them. Where a proxy holder purports to vote in a manner contrary to the instructions given in the proxy form, without any apparent justification for so doing, the chairman or scrutineers should note specifically the proxies concerned, and if the figures affect, or could affect, the result of the resolution, application should be made to the court to determine whether the votes be accepted as cast, accepted as the form of proxy directed, or rejected.

Two conflicting principles of law arise in connection with proxies, and a chairman may sometimes find it difficult to decide whether to accept or reject a vote which a person claims to exercise as a proxy. The first principle is that it is the duty of the chairman to obtain, if possible, the decision of the members. The second is that, since the right to appoint a proxy is given by contract, that is, the contract constituted by the articles, any member who seeks to exercise the right to appoint a proxy must carry out and comply with whatever the articles specify. In accordance with the first principle, it has been decided[35] that where articles prescribed that proxies must be in a specified form or as near thereto as circumstances should permit, and the specified form was a proxy applicable to a single meeting, general proxies were permissible.

On the other hand, where particular formalities are prescribed they must be followed. If they are not, it is not merely the chairman's right, but his or her duty, as representing the shareholders, to reject them. One formality usually required by the articles is that forms of proxy be deposited with the company in advance of the meeting. The usual requirement is for the deposit to be made not less than 48 hours before the meeting (see, for example, reg 62 of Table A). The Act prohibits a longer period from being specified (s 372(5)). The importance of strictly complying with formalities specified in the articles as to place or time of deposit or the form of address on an envelope is illustrated by *Burnett v Gill*.[36] In this case, the articles provided that no person should be entitled to vote as a proxy unless the instrument appointing that person was deposited at the office of the company 48 hours before the meeting. The company's registered office was the office of the secretary, a chartered accountant. It was held that a proxy addressed to 'The Chairman of the Meeting, c/o The Secretary' whose name only was mentioned, was not duly deposited at the office.

---

35   *Isaacs v Chapman* (1915) 32 TLR 183.
36   (1906) *The Times*, June 13.

In *Harben v Phillips*,[37] Cotton LJ explained the principle which justifies requiring compliance with formalities in the articles: 'The right of a shareholder to vote by proxy depends on the contract between himself and his co-shareholders, and where parties have a right depending upon the contract between them and the other parties, then, in my opinion, all the requisitions of the contract as to the exercise of the right must be followed.' In that case, it was held that the proxy papers which were not attested as required by the articles were improperly admitted by the chairman. Presumably, even though the right of members of a company limited by shares to appoint a proxy is now conferred by the Act, the articles may still validly require attestation of the proxies. If they do, the person appointed as proxy cannot act as an attesting witness.[38]

Articles may provide that a vote given in accordance with the terms of an instrument of proxy is to be regarded as valid, notwithstanding the death or insanity of the principal, or revocation of the proxy or authority under which it was executed, or the transfer of the share under which it was given, unless notice of the event giving rise to the invalidity is received at the registered office before the meeting or adjourned meeting at which the proxy is to be used. In *Cousins v International Brick Co*,[39] the articles contained a similar provision, but it was held that a member who had given a proxy and had not revoked it could attend the meeting personally and vote, in which case his proxy could not vote for him. The provision for revocation by a transfer is a dangerous one: in order to give it any meaning, the word 'transfer' must mean something less than registration. If so, sending of a transfer form to the company constitutes notice of the transfer and the result will be that, until the transfer is registered, the shares concerned may be disenfranchised. The transferor remains on the register but is treated as having revoked any proxy which he or she had given previously. The transferee may be unable to obtain a fresh proxy from the transferor, who by that time will probably not be concerned as to whether the votes are exercised or not.

Difficult problems frequently arise as to which of two or more proxies is valid. It is sometimes thought that a later proxy automatically revokes an earlier one, but this is not so. There are two facets to the problem: the first, what was the intention of the appointor; the second, what is the evidence of the intention. As to intention, it will normally be the intention of a person who makes a new appointment that a former appointment be revoked and replaced by the new one, but this will not necessarily be the case. The appointor may forget about the earlier proxy; the appointor may intend that both appointments should be effective, perhaps in order to increase his or her voting rights; the appointor may think that he or she is required to fill up the form which has been sent to him or her; or the appointor may wish to confuse the matter for the sake of confusion. As to the evidence of the intention, there is usually

---

37   (1883) 23 ChD 14 at 32.
38   *Re Parrott* [1891] 2 QB 151.
39   [1931] 2 Ch 90.

none except perhaps a date on the form of proxy or the date when it is received. But with modern postal delays, date of receipt is little guide, and dates on the forms themselves are by no means conclusive. The matter may be further complicated if an earlier proxy is stated to be irrevocable, or if the company is on notice that it was given, irrevocably, for valuable consideration.

The problem should be avoided as far as possible by some provision in the articles, but in the absence of that, the following guidelines are offered to enable a chairman or scrutineer to decide on proxy problems, where the problem is not covered by the articles:

(a) If there are two or more proxies for the same member or the same shares, the later in date (if given) should be accepted to the exclusion of the earlier.

(b) If there is no date, the one which appears on the evidence to have been signed later should be accepted to the exclusion of the others.

(c) If there is no sufficient evidence, and both proxy holders claim the right to vote, they should both be excluded since neither can establish the right.

(d) If a later proxy is received too late to be used at the meeting, it will, nevertheless, constitute notice of revocation of the earlier proxy. If the meeting is adjourned, or a poll is held later, the later proxy may be valid for that purpose.

(e) If the earlier proxy, in any of the above cases, was made irrevocable for valuable consideration and the proxy holder claims that he or she is still entitled to the vote, that claim should be recognised as being the valid compliance with the requirements of the articles for voting by proxy. A shareholder must not be assumed to intend to commit a breach of the contract with the earlier proxy holder, and any later proxy should be rejected so long as the first proxy holder claims the right to vote.

(f) If the member is personally present at the meeting, this presence will not of itself revoke the authority given to the proxy. If the member seeks to vote, this will displace his or her proxy on that resolution, but the authority revives for subsequent purposes unless, once again, the member acts to displace the proxy's authority.

It has been decided that if the articles provide that a proxy shall be valid, notwithstanding that it has been revoked, unless notice of revocation is received before the meeting then that provision shall mean what it says. Accordingly, a revocation notice received after the commencement of the meeting but before a poll is taken is ineffective.[40] If, however, the member votes in person, this will constitute valid revocation.[41]

A proxy for a specified meeting is not available for a different meeting. This will be so even if the specified meeting never takes place and another meeting is called

---

40 *Spiller v Mayo* [1926] WN 78.
41 *Cousins v International Brick Co Ltd* [1931] 2 Ch 90.

instead, perhaps for identical business. A similar type of issue arose in *Oliver v Dalgleish*[42] where forms of proxy were given to X by a number of shareholders for a meeting to be held on a particular day. The forms described the meeting as an annual general meeting whereas it was in fact an extraordinary general meeting. Some of the forms instructed X to vote against the resolutions. X simply marked his voting paper 'for' the resolutions without stating how many votes he cast. The chairman rejected all his votes. It was held (a) that the misdescription of the meeting did not invalidate the forms of proxy, and (b) that the failure to obey the instructions of some of those who gave the proxies did not invalidate all the votes cast by X, who should be taken to have cast in favour of the resolutions all those votes which he was authorised so to use. The more difficult question, as to what to do with the votes instructed to be cast against the resolution; did not arise since they were insufficient to affect the outcome of the vote.

An adjourned meeting, as regards notice, is regarded in law as a continuance of the original meeting.[43] Consequently, where the articles require proxies to be lodged before the meeting this means the original meeting.[44] Normally, articles require the lodging before the meeting or adjourned meeting at which the votes are sought to be cast. In that case, lodging by the specified time before the adjourned meeting meets is effective; but this is only effective if the meeting is in fact adjourned. *Shaw v Tati Concessions*[45] makes it clear that if all that happens is that directions are given for a poll to be taken at a later time, but the meeting itself is not adjourned, the provision does not take effect so as to validate the proxy. The mere postponement of the poll is not an adjournment ad hoc of the meeting within the meaning of an article allowing the lodgement of proxies 48 hours before a meeting or adjourned meeting. The original meeting continues for the purpose of the poll, and no fresh proxies may be lodged.

The problem of *Shaw v Tati Concessions* will not arise where the articles permit lodging of proxies a certain period of time before the taking of a poll (rather than a certain period of time before the meeting). Articles frequently provide that proxies may be lodged not less than 24 hours before a poll (see, for example, Table A, reg 62(b)(c)). If this is so, there may be proxies which were too late (within 48 hours before the meeting) for effect in full at the meeting, for example to join in demanding a poll, but which are in time for being used if a poll is demanded and held.

---

42 [1963] 1 WLR 1274.
43 *Scadding v Lorant* (1851) 3 HLC 418.
44 *McLaren v Thomson* [1917] 2 Ch 261.
45 [1913] 1 Ch 292.

Chapter 10

ADJOURNMENTS OF MEMBERS' MEETINGS

GENERAL PRINCIPLES

(1) Procedure on adjournment

When a meeting is adjourned, it is customary to fix the day and time for the adjourned meeting. Notice of an adjourned meeting, where it is adjourned to a fixed date, is not necessary unless the articles otherwise provide. This is because the adjourned meeting is treated as merely a continuation of the original meeting. Business is therefore confined to that specified in the original notice.[1] However, notwithstanding the rule that the adjourned meeting is considered a continuation of the original, resolutions passed at the adjourned meeting are treated as passed on the date of the adjourned meeting.

However, reg 45 in Table A provides for a fresh notice to be given if the adjournment is for 14 days or more. In this case, the regulation requires that seven clear days' notice be given, specifying the time and place of the meeting and the general nature of the business to be transacted. In some instances, articles differ from Table A in that they require notice to be given of adjourned meetings but do not specify the notice period. In such cases, the same notice must be given as for the original meeting. It is therefore clear that, if the meeting is the annual general meeting, or if the remaining business includes a special resolution, 21 clear days' notice will be required.

It is unclear how much notice would have to be given in such a case if the original business of an extraordinary general meeting included special resolutions but all that remained for consideration at the adjourned meeting were ordinary resolutions, which normally require only 14 clear days' notice. It is suggested that the same 21 days' notice as was given for the original meeting should still be given.

Where no provision is made by the articles as to the adjournment of a meeting, the power of adjourning is vested in the meeting.[2] The chairman cannot adjourn the meeting without its authority. If he or she purports to do so, the meeting may proceed in any event. Motions for adjournment can generally be brought forward at

---

1   *Kerr v Wilkie* (1860) 1 LT 501.
2   Cf *R v Grimshaw* (1847) 11 Jur 965; *Stoughton v Reynolds* (1736) 2 Strange 1044.

any period of the meeting, and take precedence over any matter then under consideration.

Usually, however, the question of adjournments is provided for by the articles, in which case the provisions of the articles must be followed. In the unusual situation where the meeting is in total disorder, so the views of the members cannot be ascertained, the chairman has an inherent power (whatever the provisions of the articles) to adjourn the meeting for a short time, taking steps, so far as possible, to ensure that all present know of the adjournment.[3] The way in which the chairman may exercise this inherent power, and the power of the court to adjourn a meeting, are discussed below.

Regulation 45 of Table A gives a common example of the type of provision which may be included in the articles with respect to adjournments. It provides that the chairman of the meeting may, with the consent of a meeting at which a quorum is present (and shall, if so directed by the meeting), adjourn the meeting from time to time and from place to place, but that no business is to be transacted at any adjourned meeting other than the business left unfinished at the meeting from which the adjournment took place. When a meeting is adjourned for 14 days or more, seven days' clear notice of the adjourned meeting is to be given specifying time, place and general nature of the business. Otherwise, notice is unnecessary. Under an article such as this the power for adjournment is given absolutely to the meeting. Sometimes, however, the articles provide only that the chairman may adjourn with the consent of the meeting, without providing that the chairman shall adjourn if directed by the meeting. In that case the chairman cannot adjourn without the consent of the meeting, but cannot be compelled to adjourn the meeting against his or her wishes.[4]

Where a meeting is inquorate then not only does it lack the power to transact business but generally it will also lack power to resolve upon an adjournment. However the relevant rules may make provision for such an eventuality. For example, reg 41 of Table A provides that, where a quorum is not attained, or ceases to exist, the meeting will be adjourned 'to the same day in the next week at the same time or place or to such time and place as the directors may determine'.

Articles (for example reg 51 of Table A) usually permit a poll to be called for a proposal to adjourn. In that event, the articles will generally provide that the poll be taken immediately, or, if they do not so provide in express terms, there must be an implied requirement for the purpose in order to give effect to the obvious intention. If a poll is taken, the proxy holders may be in doubt whether or not they can exercise their proxy votes, and if so, how. In some situations, it will be plain how they should exercise the votes, as being in the best interests of their appointors.[5]

---

3   *John v Rees* [1970] Ch 345; *Byng v London Life Association Ltd* [1989] BCLC 400.
4   *Salisbury Gold Mining Co v Hathorn* [1897] AC 268.
5   See *Re Waxed Papers Ltd* (1937) 2 All ER 481.

Sometimes, they will have been given specific directions for this purpose, but in other cases they may be in doubt. A proxy holder should act on the principle that he or she is an agent for the appointor, and, in the absence of express instructions, is entitled to act in whatever way he or she feels is in the interests of the appointor or accords with what the appointor would wish. If the proxy holder takes a decision in accordance with that view, held in good faith, it will not be open to successful challenge by the appointor, the company or anyone else. If the proxy holder feels unable to decide, he or she may take no action. The agency is in the proxy holder personally; even if the proxy was canvassed by the board, it is the proxy, and not the board, who has the right and duty to decide.[6]

The directors of a company, in the absence of express authority in the articles of association, have no power to postpone a general meeting of the company properly convened.[7] If they endeavour to exercise such a power, the shareholders can, if they think fit, meet at the place, time and day appointed by the notice and transact all the business which could properly be put before the meeting as convened. If the directors wish to postpone a meeting, the only way is to meet formally and to persuade the meeting to adjourn itself to a more suitable and convenient time.

It is common for directors to wish to postpone a meeting, either because circumstances have changed or changes are expected. In such situations they should, if time permits, inform shareholders of their intention to postpone the meeting and the reason for this, either by circular or, where time is too short, by newspaper advertisement. The purpose of notifying shareholders is to indicate that the meeting will be a mere formality and it will be a waste of the shareholders' time to attend the meeting.

Finally, it should be noted that a meeting may, in certain circumstances, be continued on a later date without any adjournment in the strict sense having taken place.[8]

(2)   Postponement of meetings

A properly convened meeting cannot be postponed. The proper course to adopt is to hold the meeting as originally intended, and then and there adjourn it to a more suitable date. If this course is not adopted, members will be entitled to ignore the notice of postponement, and, if sufficient to form a quorum, hold the meeting as originally convened and validly transact the business thereat.

---

6   See further on proxies, Chapter 9.
7   *Smith v Paringa Mines* [1906] 2 Ch 193.
8   *Jackson v Hamlyn* [1953] 1 Ch 577.

EXERCISE OF THE CHAIRMAN'S POWER TO ADJOURN

The power to adjourn, given to the chairman either by the articles or inherently, is a fiduciary one. The chairman is not entitled to adjourn a meeting capriciously before the business of the meeting has been transacted, and if the chairman purports to do so without good reason, the meeting may appoint another chairman and proceed with the business.[9] Similarly, the chairman may not adjourn to a place or time which would be unreasonable for shareholders. Since the chairman's power is fiduciary, it will sometimes be the chairman's duty to adjourn. If, for example, he or she believes that shareholders should be given an opportunity to reconsider a proposal, or to consider an alternative, or to review the matter in the light of changed circumstances, the chairman should exercise the power to adjourn and should explain why the power is so exercised.

The inherent power of the chairman to adjourn was considered by the Court of Appeal in *Byng v London Life Association Ltd.*[10] The article considered in this case was consistent with reg 45 of Table A, that is, it gave the chairman, with the consent of a quorate meeting, the power to adjourn. The Court of Appeal held that, if it was not possible for the chairman to validly ascertain the views of the meeting, such an article would not interfere with the chairman's fundamental common law duty to ensure that all who are entitled to be heard and to vote are given the opportunity to do so and the chairman's consequential residual common law power to adjourn the meeting. The reason that it had become impossible to proceed with the meeting and impossible to ascertain the views of the members as to adjournment in *Byng* was that the meeting was being held in a series of rooms which were supposedly linked by audio-visual means. However, the audio-visual system broke down and it became impossible to communicate adequately between the rooms. While the Court of Appeal upheld the residual common law power of the chairman to adjourn in these circumstances, it held that it was not sufficient that the chairman merely exercised the power of adjournment in good faith. Rather, the power must be exercised upon the basis of the principles laid down in *Associated Provincial Picture Houses Ltd v Wednesbury Corporation*[11] for the proper exercise of a discretion. In the context of company meetings, this means:

> 'The chairman's decision will not be declared invalid unless on the facts which he knew or ought to have known he failed to take into account all relevant factors or reached a conclusion which no reasonable chairman, properly directing himself as to his duties could have reached.'[12]

---

9   *National Dwellings Society v Sykes* [1894] 3 Ch 159.
10 [1989] BCLC 400.
11 [1948] 1 KB 223.
12 [1989] BCLC 400 at 419, per Browne-Wilkinson LJ.

On the facts of the case, the chairman's behaviour in adjourning the meeting had not conformed with this principle. The reason for this was that the chairman had neglected to take into account a number of matters relevant to the exercise of his discretion to adjourn. These matters included the objections of members to the adjournment of the meeting to that afternoon; the fact that any members unable to attend the adjourned afternoon meeting in person would not be able to vote by proxy since it was too late for them to lodge their proxies; and the fact that the chairman was wrong in believing that it was necessary for the company to pass a special resolution on that day.

THE COURT'S POWER TO ADJOURN

There are circumstances in which the court has a power to adjourn a company meeting. Such a power may be exercised where, for example, circulars sent to shareholders by the directors with the notice of the meeting are misleading.[13]

BUSINESS AT ADJOURNED MEETINGS

Section 381 provides that where a resolution is passed at an adjourned meeting of a company, or a similar meeting of the holders of any class of shares of a company, or of the directors of a company, the resolution shall for all purposes be treated as having been passed on the date on which it was in fact passed and shall not be deemed to have been passed on any earlier date.

The articles usually provide what business may be conducted at an adjourned meeting. Usually, only business which could properly have been transacted at the original meeting, had it not been postponed, can be transacted at the adjourned meeting (see, for example, Table A, reg 45). Sometimes, however, it is possible to transact business which could not have been transacted at the original meeting. Thus in *Catesby v Burnett*,[14] the articles provided that a member should not be qualified to be elected a director unless 14 clear days' notice of the intention to so elect the member was given to the company before the day of election. At the date of the annual general meeting there were two directors due for retirement, but the meeting was adjourned without any election of directors. Notice had been given 14 clear days before the adjourned meeting, and the two new directors elected at that meeting were held to be validly appointed, since the date of the adjourned meeting was the day of election. If the articles had provided for 14 days' notice before the meeting at which they were elected (rather than 14 days' notice before the day of election), the election would not have been valid.

---

13   *Northern Counties Securities v Jackson* [1974] 1 WLR 1133.
14   [1916] 2 Ch 325.

For similar reasons, proxies will sometimes be available for use at an adjourned meeting where they would not have been available at the earlier meeting, as, for example, where they have to be deposited not less than 48 hours 'before meeting or adjourned meeting' (see reg 62(a) of Table A).

An adjourned meeting is in law the continuance of the original meeting,[15] and a fresh notice is not therefore necessary,[16] unless the articles require such a notice to be given. Most articles do so provide where the adjournment is of some length (for example, Table A, reg 45).

---

15   *Scadding v Lorant* (1851) 3 HLC 418.
16   *Wills v Murray* (1850) 4 Ex 843.

Chapter 11

MEETINGS OF DIRECTORS

INTRODUCTION

Section 282 provides that every company registered on or after 1 November 1929 (other than a private company) shall have at least two directors, and every company registered before that date and every private company shall have at least one director.

Normal day-to-day management decisions are taken by directors and others with responsibility in that field delegated by the board. Some matters must be dealt with in a more formal way, with a record kept of any decisions, and for this purpose board meetings are held. Almost invariably, the articles contain provisions relating to board meetings. For example, reg 88 of Table A provides that, subject to the other articles, the directors may regulate their meetings as they think fit; that questions arising at any meeting shall be decided by a majority of votes; that in case of an equality of votes the chairman shall have a second or casting vote; that a director may, and the secretary on the requisition of a director shall, at any time summon a meeting of the directors; and that it shall not be necessary to give notice of a meeting of directors to any director for the time being absent from the UK. Further regulations on the proceedings of directors are contained in regs 89 to 98, and some of these are discussed below.

In considering the activities of directors discussed in this chapter (and in this book generally), it should always be borne in mind that directors hold their powers in a fiduciary capacity and must exercise them bona fide for the benefit of the company, not for their own ends and for 'proper purposes' (ie for the purposes for which they were conferred).[1]

CHAIRMAN

To constitute a valid board meeting the proper person must be in the chair.

The appointment of the chairman is generally governed by the articles. Regulation 91 of Table A, for example, provides that the directors may elect a chairman of

---

1   *Piercy v S Mills & Co* [1920] 1 Ch 77.

their meetings and determine the period for which the chairman is to hold office, and that if no such chairman is elected, if the chairman is unwilling to preside, or if at any meeting the chairman is not present within five minutes after the time appointed for holding the meeting, the directors present may choose one of their number to be chairman of the meeting.

The election of a chairman may be a general one or merely for a particular meeting. It is important that a clear record of this is kept in the minutes, since confusion and dispute will often result if it is not clear whether there is a regular chairman, especially if the articles give the chairman a casting vote. Moreover, confusion may be compounded by the fact that reg 91 requires no particular formality for the resignation of the chairman.[2]

An appointment of a chairman of directors made in contravention of the articles is void and is not regularised by mere acquiescence, and consequently resolutions carried by the casting vote of such a chairman are inoperative.[3]

PROPER CONSTITUTION OF THE BOARD

Subject to what is said below concerning s 35A, acts done as directors by persons who have not been validly elected do not bind the company.[4] It may be otherwise if the fact that they were not properly elected is only discovered afterwards, for s 285 provides that the acts of a director or manager shall be valid notwithstanding any defect that may afterwards be discovered in his or her appointment or qualification. This section is merely intended to cure slips in the appointment of directors and cannot in any case be relied on by a person who in fact knew of the invalidity even if its discovery was not general, or when there was no appointment at all.[5]

Outsiders are, in the absence of knowledge to the contrary, entitled to assume that the domestic affairs of a company are properly conducted, the basis for this principle being known as the rule in *Royal British Bank v Turquand*.[6] It is outside the scope of this book to consider the present importance of this rule, but it seems that it is of minimal importance since the introduction of s 35A. The reason for this is that s 35A makes the acts of the directors binding on the company in favour of a person dealing with it in good faith, notwithstanding any constitutional limitations on the directors' powers. Knowing that an act is beyond the power of the directors does not show bad faith (s 35A(2)(b)). The effect of this provision seems to be to make concerns about the proper constitution of the board relevant in most cases only to internal disputes and then subject only to s 285.

---

2   *Cane v Jones* [1981] 1 All ER 533.
3   *Clark v Workman* [1920] 1 IR 107.
4   *Garden Gully United Mining Co v McLister* (1875) 1 App Cas 39.
5   *Morris v Kanssen* [1946] AC 459.
6   (1856) 6 E&B 327.

Sometimes articles provide for alternate or substitute directors to act for directors going abroad or otherwise unable to attend board meetings. Invariably, an alternate may be either an existing director or, if he is not, must be approved by resolution of the directors (Table A, reg 65). Under normal articles, one person may be alternate for more than one director, but it may be thought desirable to exclude such a possibility by expressly stating that one person may not be alternate for more than one director. An alternate director is counted as a director, and if the alternate is a director in his or her own right he or she counts as two persons, both for the purposes of quorum and of voting. Depending on the articles, it may be possible for one person to constitute a meeting if that person is duly appointed alternate for a sufficient number of directors to form a quorum.

It is important to recognise that, under most articles an alternate director is not deemed to be the agent of the director appointing him. Instead, he is deemed for all purposes to be a director. This means that he 'shall alone be responsible for his own acts and defaults' (Table A, reg 69).

An alternate director appointed pursuant to an article in such terms is therefore subject to all the duties and responsibilities which apply to a full director. He should, for example, ensure that his acts and decisions as an alternate director are made in the best interests of the company; he should notify or declare his interests in contracts or arrangements to the board under s 317; he should be entered in the company's registers as a director and his appointment notified to Companies House (s 288). Particularly, he should not act or vote blindly in accordance with instructions given to him by his appointor.

DIRECTORS' OBLIGATION TO MEET

Where board approval is required, directors must either act at a duly constituted meeting or by unanimous decision arrived at informally.[7] This requirement of a board meeting was illustrated starkly in *Barber's Case*.[8] The articles provided that no person not recommended by the board of directors for election as a director should be eligible unless at the time that person had held 20 shares for two months. B, who was not a shareholder, was elected unanimously at a general meeting, six out of seven directors, who were then the only shareholders, being present. It was held that B's election was void. 'Six directors out of seven met in a different capacity and for a different purpose, and such a meeting does not make them a board of directors.'[9]

---

7   *Collie's Claim* (1871) 12 Eq 246, 258; *ex parte Kennedy* (1890) 44 ChD 472 at 481.
8   *Re East Norfolk Tramways Co, Barber's Case* (1877) 5 ChD 963.
9   Ibid at 697.

A board meeting can be held under informal circumstances but, for example, a casual meeting of the only two directors of a company at a railway station cannot be treated as a board meeting at the option of one against the will of the other.[10] The dividing line is, however, narrow. Where one of the only two directors did not attend a meeting, proper notice of which had been given, but was met by the other director shortly after in the passage, that other director proposed a resolution and, on the first director objecting, declared it passed by virtue of his casting vote, and this resolution was held to have been duly passed.[11] In any case, a subsequent meeting can ratify the business done at an informal meeting.[12] It can also ratify an unauthorised act of an agent of the company.[13]

Articles frequently allow the directors, if unanimous, to act without holding a meeting. Regulation 93 of Table A provides that a resolution in writing, signed by all the directors entitled to receive notice of a meeting of the directors, shall be as valid and effectual as if it had been passed at a meeting of the directors duly convened and held.

In the event that the number of directors entitled to receive notice is less than the number of directors required to constitute a quorum (eg because a number of directors are overseas and therefore not entitled to notice under the articles) it appears that a resolution passed pursuant to an article in terms of reg 93 (or its predecessor, reg 106 in the 1948 Table A) will not be valid; *Hood Sailmakers Ltd v Axford*.[14] The members of the board in the UK cannot pass resolutions in writing in the absence of overseas colleagues unless the UK directors constitute a quorum in their own right.

In the case of a company with a sole director it might be thought that the common law rule that one person cannot, in general, constitute a meeting would preclude the company from holding board meetings. Instead, best practice would be for the sole director to record decisions (which would, in the event that there had been more than one director, have been considered at a board meeting) as resolutions in writing, signed by the sole director. However, in *Neptune (Vehicle Washing Equipment) Ltd v Fitzgerald* the court considered the application of s 317 to companies with a sole director. In that case a sole director purported to hold a meeting at which he resolved to terminate his own contract of employment and authorise payment to himself of £100,892.62 allegedly due to him under that contract. The payment was then made and he retired as director.

Subsequently the company (under new management and ownership) sought to recover the sum paid by way of summary judgment. The former director appealed

---

10   *Barron v Porter* [1914] 1 Ch 895.
11   *Smith v Paringa Mines* [1906] 2 Ch 193.
12   *Re Portuguese Consolidated Copper Mines* (1889) 42 ChD 160.
13   *Molineaux v London, Birmingham etc Co* [1902] 2 KB 589.
14   [1997] 1 WLR 625.

against the summary judgment and was given leave to defend. In the course of the appeal the court considered the application of s 317 which requires a director who is, in any way, whether directly or indirectly interested in a contract or proposed contract (or other arrangement or transaction) with the company to declare the nature of his or her interest at a meeting of the company.

The court held that the words of the section required that a meeting of the sole director was required in order that he could make the declaration required by s 317. If no other person was in attendance the declaration could be made by the director to himself – 'although not necessarily aloud'. If another person was in attendance, such as the secretary, it should be made aloud in the hearing of those attending.

The court further held that the declaration, whether made aloud or not, should be recorded in the minutes of the meeting – although omission of such a minute was not conclusive as to whether the declaration had in fact been made or not.

Implicit in the court's decision is the assumption that a sole director can constitute a meeting – at least in circumstances where there is a statutory provision which appears to require a board meeting to be held.

The decision appears to have been driven by the court's assumption that the underlying rationale for s 317 is that the declaration should be a distinct event and there should be a 'statutory pause for thought' in cases where a director was interested in a particular matter. During the pause for thought the (director and the) board should consider the possibility that the director concerned might, by virtue of the matter under consideration be in breach of his duties to the company, or at greater risk of committing such a breach in the future. The court also appeared struck by the need for such a declaration to be recorded in writing.

The decision stretches the usual definitions of both a 'meeting' and of a 'declaration'. An approach which demands less elasticity from such terms and which appears to satisfy both the requirement for a 'statutory pause for thought' and a written record of it might be to ensure that, wherever a s 317 declaration is required, it should be made aloud by the director to himself and also recorded by way of written resolution. However, s 317 does seem to require a board meeting. Faced with the inconsistency between the Act and the usual common law rule that one person may not constitute a meeting, prudence dictates that the sole director should purport to hold a board meeting at which to make his or her declaration, should ensure that the declaration is a distinct event at that meeting, should pause for thought sufficient to satisfy the statute and should ensure that all of this is sufficiently minuted.

A director need not attend every meeting, though he or she should attend as often as circumstances permit. Ultimately, in the event of an insolvency, a director must be able to protect himself against allegations of, for example, wrongful trading under s 214 of the Insolvency Act 1986. A director is bound to use fair and reasonable diligence in the management of the company's affairs and to act honestly.[15] A director is not, however, liable for misfeasance committed by co-directors without his or her knowledge at a board meeting at which he or she is not present.[16]

NOTICE OF MEETINGS

Directors of a company can, at any meeting of the board, deal with all the affairs of the company then requiring attention so far as the powers conferred on them by the articles extend; previous notice of special business is not necessary[17] unless the articles so require.

Reasonable notice must be given of the meeting, but it need not be in writing unless the articles so provide.[18] Even in the absence of a provision such as that contained in reg 88 of Table A, presumably any director may summon a meeting. What is reasonable notice will depend on the facts in any particular case. If a practice develops giving a certain length of notice this will be held to be reasonable in the absence of any particular circumstances which would make such a conclusion invalid. In *Re Homer Gold Mines*,[19] a shorter notice than any previously given was held invalid, since the court came to the conclusion that the notice had been so given with a view to excluding certain directors. A notice may, however, be extremely short if all the directors are able to attend and if any director wishes to object to the shortness of the notice that director should make such an objection at once.[20]

It might well be thought that failure to give proper notice to each director will invalidate all proceedings at the meeting (unless all the directors do attend).[21] But although the matter is not free from doubt, it seems that a director who does not receive proper notice merely has the right to a second meeting if that director does not attend the first; that the failure of that director to seek a second meeting within a reasonable time of discovering the first will amount to a waiver of that right; and that in this event the proceedings of the meeting become effectively unchallengeable.[22] There is, however, no need to send notice when the directors have decided to hold meetings at regular intervals, that is, when there is a fixed day and time of

---

15 *Re Forest of Dean Coal Mining Co* (1878) 10 ChD 450; *Re City Equitable Fire Insurance Co* [1925] Ch 407.
16 *Perry's Case* (1876) 34 LT 716.
17 *La Compagnie de Mayville v Whitley* [1896] 1 Ch 788.
18 *Browne v La Trinidad* (1887) 37 ChD 1.
19 (1888) 39 ChD 546.
20 *Browne v La Trinidad* (1887) 37 ChD 1.
21 *Re Homer Gold Mines Ltd* (1888) 39 ChD 546; *Harben v Phillips* (1883) 23 ChD 14.
22 *Browne v La Trinidad* (1887) 37 ChD 1 (10 minutes' notice not specifying the business); *Bentley-Stevens v Jones* (1974) 1 WLR 638 (notice sent of meeting the following day and not received because director away from home until the evening of that day).

which all directors have knowledge, and therefore, notice (for example, weekly meetings on Fridays at 3 pm or every first Thursday in the month at 11 am). Even in the absence of a provision as to directors out of the UK similar to reg 88 of Table A, in certain circumstances notice need not be given to a director who is abroad and out of reach.[23] A director cannot, however, waive in advance his or her right to notice and even if the director says, 'I shall not be able to come, you need not summon me', he or she must be given notice.[24]

Notice must be given even if the director indicates that he will not attend. In *Re Portuguese Consolidated Copper Mines*[25] a director of a company, on being told a meeting would be held next week, said 'I cannot be there'. It was held that this could not be relied on as a waiver of his right to notice.

Perhaps if a director were at such a distance that it would be absolutely impossible for him to attend then the secretary might be excused for not giving notice to the director and the meeting would be properly convened? Possibly the same exception might apply when a director was so dangerously ill that he could not be moved.[26] However, such exceptions are unlikely to hold good except on very particular facts in very particular cases. It is therefore highly desirable to give notice to all directors for all meetings – even to those who may be abroad and whatever the company's knowledge of their intentions, or state of health or other circumstances.

Where notice is required to be sent to a director under the articles, the notice must still be given even though it cannot possibly reach the director until after the meeting has taken place.

The notice convening the meeting should, in most cases, provide a sufficient description of the nature of the business which the meeting is to transact, and the meeting cannot in ordinary cases go outside the business described in that notice.[27]

In some cases the practice is not to give any indication of the nature of the business, unless there is something unusual to be considered. For example, notices of meetings of directors in many companies contain no agenda.

In other cases the articles may provide that the nature of any business to be transacted, other than routine business, must be specified but this is unusual in the case of directors' meetings.

---

23 *Re Halifax Sugar Co* (1890) 62 LT 564.
24 *Re Portuguese Consolidated Copper Mines* (1889) 42 ChD 160.
25 (1889) 42 ChD 160.
26 *Young v Ladies' Imperial Club* [1920] 2 KB 523. If a meeting may legitimately be summoned in an emergency, it may be enough for those convening it to serve notice on all members who can with proper effort be found: *MacLelland v NUJ* [1975] ICR 116 at 135.
27 *Longfield Parish Council v Wright* (1919) 88 LJ (Ch) 119.

The object of requiring a proper notice of the purposes for which the meeting is to be held is to enable a person entitled to attend to exercise his or her own judgment as to whether to attend. A notice may be good in part and bad in part and it is not wholly invalid because it extends to something which cannot be done at the meeting.[28] The heading in a notice of 'Any other business' will generally authorise the transaction of business of a purely formal nature but not business of any substantial importance. In *Young v Ladies' Imperial Club*,[29] it was held that, as the notice of a meeting did not state the object of the meeting with sufficient particularity, it was invalid and consequently the proceedings of that meeting were invalidated.

If an agenda is required and/or drawn up,it should enable those entitled to attend to ascertain what matters will be discussed and, if circulated beforehand, give them an opportunity for forming some opinion as to the course which they will adopt at the meeting. A properly drawn up agenda prevents many questions being put to the chair, considerably shortens a meeting, and helps to get the sense of the meeting in an intelligent and expeditious manner. Further, a well-arranged agenda prevents confusion and irritation which may be caused by directors speaking on insufficient information. It is generally advisable to consult the chairman of the meeting in preparing the agenda.

QUORUM

(1) General rules

Business can only be validly transacted by the majority of the directors at a meeting properly convened[30] and held, and at which there is a quorum as prescribed by the articles. Regulation 89 of Table A provides that the quorum necessary for the transaction of the business of the directors may be fixed by the directors, and unless so fixed shall be two. Under a provision such as this, one director who is also alternate for another could constitute a quorum for a meeting. The articles may also provide that one director can constitute a quorum in any case.[31] If no provision on quorum is made by the articles, a majority of the directors will constitute a quorum, but under certain circumstances apparently the necessary number may be determined by the practice of the board.[32]

A quorum of directors means a quorum competent to transact and vote on the business before the board. Therefore, in *Yuill v Greymouth Point Elizabeth R Co*,[33]

---

28   *Cleve v Financial Corporation* (1873) LR 16 Eq 363.
29   [1920] 2 KB 523.
30   *York Tramways Co v Willows* (1882) 8 QBD 685.
31   *Re Fireproof Doors* [1916] 2 Ch 142.
32   *Regent's Canal Ironworks* [1867] WN 79.
33   [1904] 1 Ch 32.

where the articles prohibited interested directors from voting, a resolution passed at a meeting of three directors, two of whom were interested in the subject matter of the resolution, was held invalid. In *Re North Eastern Insurance Co*,[34] articles provided that directors could contract with the company, but should not vote in connection with such contracts, and that until otherwise determined three should be a quorum. Four directors were present at a meeting. At that meeting a resolution was passed for the issue of a debenture to one of the directors present, who did not vote on that resolution, and a similar resolution was passed to issue another debenture to another director who was present, but did not vote on this latter resolution. It was held in the circumstances of the case that the issue of both debentures was part of one entire transaction in which the directors to whom the debentures were issued were jointly interested and that there was therefore no quorum and the debentures were not validly issued. It was subsequently resolved that in future a quorum should be two so as to remove the difficulty. One of the directors interested in the transaction was one of the three directors present when that resolution was passed and being interested was unable to count towards a quorum. The purported reduction of the quorum was consequently ineffective. The principle that those who are not entitled to vote on a resolution at a board meeting cannot form part of the quorum is embodied in reg 95 of Table A, although these cases make it clear that the principle stands even in the absence of such an article.

(2) Abuse of quorum provisions

It seems that in certain circumstances the court will be prepared to step in and make an appropriate order where a director refuses to attend and thus deprives the board meeting of a quorum. An example of this occurred in *Re Copal Varnish Co*,[35] where one director out of a board of two refused to attend meetings summoned to consider transfers of shares in order to prevent a quorum being formed. It was held that the transferees were entitled to an order directing the company to register the transfers, since a shareholder has a property in his or her shares which he or she has the right to dispose of subject only to an express restriction in the articles. Even if the articles give directors a power to decline to register a transfer, such a power is not exercised where the directors have not passed a resolution declining so to register.[36]

(3) Failure to keep quorum

Where there is a quorum at the beginning of a meeting, but some of the directors leave the meeting, so that a number less than the quorum remain, any subsequent acts are invalid. This would not be the case if the articles provided that 'the quorum shall be two directors present when the meeting proceeds to business', as was

---

34 [1919] 1 Ch 198.
35 [1917] 2 Ch 349.
36 *Re Hackney Pavilion* [1924] 1 Ch 276.

found in relation to general meetings in *Re Hartley Baird*,[37] but such a provision would be most unusual. The normal provision is similar to that found in reg 89 of Table A referred to above.

(4) Minimum number of directors

Articles usually fix what is to be the maximum and minimum number of the directors. Where a minimum is fixed, and the number of the directors has never reached the minimum, they cannot act even though they are sufficient to form a quorum.[38] However, if there have been sufficient directors to satisfy the requirement of the minimum number, and their number falls below the minimum but there are nevertheless sufficient directors to form a quorum, the articles may provide that the directors continue to be entitled to act (see, for example, Table A, reg 90). However, where the number of remaining directors falls below the quorum then the articles generally give the continuing directors only very limited powers. Regulation 90 of Table A, for example, gives the continuing directors in these circumstances power only to fill vacancies or to call a general meeting. Under such an article, a single director may be entitled to act for those purposes.[39]

DIRECTORS' VOTES

(1) General

Unless the articles otherwise provide, each director has only one vote at a board meeting, and in the event of a disagreement the majority view will prevail, though the chairman is usually given a casting vote (see, for example, Table A, reg 88). In some circumstances, there may be a departure from the usual provision that decisions will be arrived at by a majority vote. For example, where there are special classes of shares each with rights to appoint directors, or where the company is, in effect, an incorporated partnership, articles frequently provide that all or some matters require an affirmative resolution from all directors, or from a specified majority, or from a majority including directors of both (or all) classes or factions.

(2) Votes of directors in matters of self-interest

Directors stand in a fiduciary relation to the company, and under the general rules relating to such a relationship a director cannot, in the absence of express provision in the articles, contract with the company without the sanction of the company in general meeting. A director is precluded from dealing on behalf of the company with himself or herself and from entering into any engagement in which he or she

---

37   [1955] Ch 143.
38   *Re Sly, Spink & Co* [1911] 2 Ch 430.
39   *Dover etc Light Railway Co* [1914] 1 Ch 568, 2 Ch 506.

has a personal interest conflicting or which may possibly conflict with the interests of the company. This rule extends not only to contracts between the company and the director but also to contracts with any firms or companies in which that director has an interest either as director or shareholder and even if the director holds the shares in the other company as a trustee. The smallest conceivable conflict of interest will be sufficient to bring this rule into operation.[40] Even the allotment of shares or the issue of debentures by directors to themselves will fall within this rule.[41] Most articles specify exemptions from this strict rule but frequently provide that in the case of any such contract the interested director is not to vote (for example, Table A, reg 94). In that case, a director prohibited from voting does not count towards a quorum (see, for example, Table A, reg 95). The articles of private companies will almost invariably vary Table A to allow directors to vote and be counted in the quorum in relation to matters in which they have an interest. In the case of companies with a sole director such variations are essential if the director is to enjoy any benefits from the company at all. In any event, prohibitions as to voting and quorum which apply to a person as director will not prevent him from voting as a shareholder at general meetings of the company upon contracts in which that director is interested,[42] and a director is entitled to attend board meetings even when that director is not entitled to vote at the board meeting.[43]

Whether any such contracts are permitted by the articles or by the Act or not[44] the provisions of s 317 must be observed. That section declares that it is the duty of a director who is in any way, whether directly or indirectly, interested in a contract or proposed contract or other arrangement or transaction with the company to declare the nature of his or her interest at a meeting of the directors of the company (s 317(1) and (5)) and provides for a fine on non-compliance with the section (s 317(7)). It appears that the strict provisions of s 317 must even be observed by a sole director.[45] It is to be noted that it is not sufficient for a director merely to declare the existence of an interest: the director must declare the nature of the interest. This does not necessarily mean the full extent or quantum of the interest. For example, if the interest that a director has is 100 shares in the other contracting company, the director must declare that he or she holds the shares but need not necessarily disclose the number. If, however, the director's shareholding in the other company were a controlling one, this fact would alter the nature of the interest held and the director would have to disclose not merely that he or she is a

---

40 *Transvaal Lands Co v New Belgium Land Co* [1914] 2 Ch 488.

41 *Neal v Quinn* (1916) WN 223.

42 *North-West Transportation Co v Beatty* (1887) 12 App Cas 589.

43 *Grimwade v BPS Syndicate* (1915) 31 TLR 531.

44 It should be stressed that certain contracts between directors (or those connected with them) and their companies are, under the Act, either generally forbidden or tightly circumscribed (see, for example, the provisions in s 320ff on substantial property transactions involving directors; and the provisions in s 330ff on loans to directors).

45 *Neptune (Vehicle Washing Equipment) Ltd v Fitzgerald (No 2)* (1995) BCC 1000. See page 92 above.

shareholder, but the controlling shareholder.[46] The principle to be observed in deciding what has to be disclosed is that any aspect of the interest which could or might affect the attitude of the director or of the other members of the board, is part of the 'nature' of the interest and must be disclosed. The articles may, however, require the director to disclose the extent of his or her interest, as well as its nature, in certain circumstances. If, for example, reg 85 of Table A applies to the company, a director may only enjoy the concessions conferred by regs 85(a) to (c) if he or she has disclosed to the directors the nature 'and extent' of any 'material' interest of his or hers.

The fact that a director discloses the nature or extent of an interest and may not vote or be counted in the quorum does not absolve that director from responsibility with regard to the proposal. The director is entitled to speak on the proposal and if he or she feels it is against the interests of the company he or she must say so. After having disclosed an interest, the director is not entitled merely to sit back and wash his or her hands of the matter.

The section also provides that in the case of a proposed contract, the declaration required by the section is to be made at the meeting of the directors at which the question of entering into the contract is first taken into consideration, or if the director is not at the date of that meeting interested in the proposed contract, at the next meeting of the directors held after the director becomes interested, and in a case where the director becomes interested in a contract after it is made, the declaration is to be made at the first meeting of the directors held after the director becomes interested (s 317(2)).

Under the section, there is deemed to be a sufficient declaration of interest if the director gives the board a general notice that he or she is a member of a specified company or firm and is to be regarded as interested in any contract which, after the date of the notice, the company may make with that company or firm, or that the director is to be regarded as interested in any contract which, after the date of the notice, the company may make with a person connected with the director within the meaning of s 346 (s 317(3)).[47] But the notice has no effect until either it is given at a meeting of the directors or the director in question takes reasonable steps to secure that it is brought up and read at the next meeting of the directors after it is given (s 317(4)).

---

46 In such circumstances he or she might (by virtue of paras 4 and 5 of Part 1 of Sch 13) also have to notify the company of his or her interest in such shares under s 324 of the Companies Act 1985.

47 Persons connected with the director include the director's spouse, children and stepchildren under 18 years of age, the director's partner, companies with which the director is associated through control of one-fifth of the nominal equity capital or voting rights, and certain trustees.

The provisions of s 317 also apply to shadow directors,[48] except that a shadow director must declare his or her interest by a notice in writing to the directors by either a specific notice in relation to a particular contract given before the date of the meeting at which a declaration would have been required by a de jure director in the same circumstances, or in the case of a general notice of interest, in the same way as required by other directors (s 317(8)).

Apart from any specific exemptions found in the articles (see, for example, Table A, reg 94) which permit a director to vote despite his or her other interests, articles usually provide in addition that the prohibitions may at any time be suspended or relaxed to any extent, and either generally or in respect of any particular contract, arrangement or transaction, by the company in general meeting (see reg 84 of Table A). However, even if the articles permit a director to vote on a resolution in which that director is interested, this does not absolve the director from disclosure, under s 317 of the nature of the interest. That disclosure has to be made so that the other directors can give due weight to the opposing interest while assessing the director's views. It is not sufficient for a director to disclose his or her interest to a mere sub-committee of the board. It must be to the full board.[49]

Articles frequently permit a director to hold any other office or place of profit under the company (other than the office of auditor) in conjunction with the office of director for such period and on such terms (as to remuneration and otherwise) as the directors may determine (see, for example, Table A, reg 84).[50] The articles usually go on to provide that, as long as disclosure of a director's interests has been made to the other directors, a director may be a party to or interested in any transaction or arrangement in which the company is interested, or may be associated with another body which is a party to a transaction or arrangement in which the company is interested (see, for example, Table A, reg 85(a) and (b)). As already discussed, the disclosure under reg 85 must, if the interest is material, include the extent, as well as the nature, of the director's interest. An article in these terms will usually go on to provide that a director so contracting or being so interested shall not be liable to account to the company for any profit realised by any such transactions or arrangement by reason of the director holding that office (for example, Table A, reg 85(c)).[51] In addition, the articles may permit a director,

---

48 The concept of 'shadow director' is defined in s 741(2) of the Companies Act 1985, as 'a person in accordance with whose directions or instructions the directors of a company are accustomed to act', although those giving advice in a professional capacity are specifically excluded. For a recent case on the definition of 'shadow director' see *Re Hydrodan (Corby) Ltd* [1994] BCC 161.

49 *Guinness plc v Saunders and Another* [1988] 1 WLR 863.

50 Subject, however, to s 319 of the Companies Act 1985 requiring the approval of a general meeting of any proposal to employ a director for more than five years when the contract is not freely terminable by the company during that period.

51 This is subject, however, to the statutory rules on directors' contracts with the company. See footnote 44 above.

notwithstanding that director's interest, to be counted in the quorum present at any meeting at which that director or any other director is appointed to hold any such office or place of profit under the company or at which the terms of any such appointment are arranged, and allow a director to vote on any such appointment or arrangement other than his or her own appointment or the arrangement of the terms of that appointment. Finally, the articles may provide that a director may act, or his or her firm may act, in a professional capacity for the company, and that the director or the director's firm shall be entitled to remuneration for professional services as if that person were not a director. However, these provisions are stated not to authorise a director or a director's firm to act as auditor to the company. Many articles (particularly those of private companies) do not contain such an elaborate provision, but it is often useful to permit the restrictions imposed by the articles to be relaxed by the company in general meeting, especially where there are only two or three directors of the company.

It should be noted that all the provisions regarding disclosure and prohibitions on voting where there is an interest apply to a wider range of matters than merely 'contract'. Section 317 applies to contracts, transactions and arrangements. Regulations 84 and 85 apply to transactions and arrangements; and reg 94, barring directors from voting at a board meeting, does so in relation to matters in which they have an interest. These wide provisions reinforce the director's fiduciary duty to disclose his or her interest in any matter which the board might consider, whether technically a contract with the company or not.

COMMITTEES

The directors may, if the articles contain the necessary authority, delegate their powers to a committee. The articles generally provide for this, as does Table A, reg 72. Where a company is regulated by an article in the form of reg 72, directors may delegate their powers to a committee of one.[52] However, a declaration made or notice given to a sub-committee of the board is not sufficient to satisfy the requirements of s 317.[53]

When a board of directors delegate their power to a committee without any provision as to the committee acting by a quorum, all acts of the committee must be done in the presence of all members of the committee, and the committee has no power to add to their number or to fill a vacancy.[54] The articles may, however, make provision for matters such as quorums for committees. Table A, reg 72, for example, provides that subject to any conditions imposed by the board, the proceedings of a committee with two or more members shall be governed so far as

---

52   See, also, *Re Fireproof Doors* (1916) 2 Ch 142.
53   *Guinness plc v Saunders and Another* [1998] 1 WLR 863.
54   *Re Liverpool Household Stores* (1890) 59 LJ Ch 616.

possible by the rules in the articles regulating the proceedings of directors. A provision like this does not remove the need to ensure that, in all cases of delegation of powers to a committee, the committee's powers and authority are clearly stated in the resolution affecting the delegation.

Committees are usually appointed for one of three main purposes: first, to deal with a matter which requires speedy decision where the whole board could not be contacted quickly enough; secondly, to deal with a matter where it is desirable to have discussion free from the embarrassing presence of a director who is personally concerned in the matter, for example for the appointment or removal of a director to or from executive office (although the minutes, as distinct from a report on the discussions, are open to inspection by directors who were not on the committee, including the one being discussed); thirdly, for routine matters such as transfer, in which case standing committees are often appointed.

The power to delegate to a committee is, like all directors' powers, a fiduciary one. It cannot be exercised for an improper purpose, for example to exclude one or more directors from the forum where the board's decisions are taken.

Chapter 12

MINUTES OF MEMBERS' AND OF BOARD MEETINGS

The purpose of minutes is to show that decisions have been taken properly and in accordance with the statutory rules, articles, operating procedures and customs of the company and the common law. For example, it must be clear from the minutes of directors' meetings that board resolutions have been taken in what the directors honestly believe to be the best interests of the company.

The minutes of a meeting should also, of course, comprise an accurate record of what was done at the meeting, for example, resolutions and decisions of the meeting should be minuted. However, it is not necessary to record the speeches or arguments in connection therewith unless that is required in order to show that, for instance, the directors are acting in the best interests of the company. Exceptionally, for example, the directors may specifically require that the reasons for making a particular decision are recorded. This may be because of the importance of the matter, because it is contentious or because the company is in a parlous financial state and the directors are particularly keen to demonstrate that their decisions are being taken in the best interests of the company and that they are not taking decisions in circumstances which might create liabilities for them under the insolvency legislation. If so, the directors' wishes must be complied with by the secretary.

The secretary's position is less clear if an individual director requests that the reasons for his or her dissent on a particular matter be recorded in the minutes. If there is any doubt among board members as to the propriety of doing so, the matter should be referred to the chairman for decision in the best interests of the company. The chairman may, if he or she is uncertain, refer the matter to the board for a decision. Again, the decision must be taken in the best interests of the company. The minutes may be drawn up during the meeting and put up for approval at the end of the meeting, but the more usual course is to approve them at the next meeting. Any inaccuracy in the minutes is fatal to their value and usefulness. The minutes should be:

(1) an exact account of what was actually agreed upon;
(2) sufficiently detailed and complete, so that a member who was absent could fully understand what was done at that meeting;
(3) concise.

The minutes should contain, inter alia:

(1) in cases where the meeting is of a comparatively small body, for example, of the board of directors of a company or of a committee of the directors, the names of those present. It is usual in the meetings of small bodies to record in the minutes the names of those persons who vote against a specific resolution, if they request this to be done;

(2) full and exact details of all contracts and questions involving financial considerations;

(3) the exact words of all resolutions which have been passed;

(4) if relevant, appointments, salaries, powers and duties of officers (these should be very explicit);

(5) instructions to officers, and all transactions authorised at that meeting.

THE OBLIGATION TO RECORD MINUTES

Section 382(1) provides that every company shall cause minutes of all proceedings of general meetings and all proceedings at meetings of its directors and where it has managers, at meetings of its managers, to be entered in books kept for that purpose. (Note, in this context, should be taken of reg 100 of Table A which imposes upon the directors the obligation to ensure that minutes are kept of the proceedings of the company, any class of shareholders, the directors or any committees of directors.) Section 382A(1) requires that written resolutions under s 381A must be recorded, along with the signatures of the members, in the same way as the minutes of a general meeting of the company. Where a company has only one member, then s 382B(1) requires that member to provide the company with a written record of any decision taken by the member which might have been taken by the company in general meeting. However, failure to comply with this requirement in relation to single member companies does not affect the validity of any decision arrived at by the single member (s 382B(3)).

THE RIGHT TO INSPECT THE MINUTES

Section 383(1) requires the minutes of proceedings of general meetings of a company to be kept at the registered office of the company and to be open to the inspection of any member without charge. The Companies (Inspection and Copying of Registers, Indexes and Documents) Regulations 1991 require the company to make the minutes available for at least two hours during business hours on each business day and to permit the person inspecting the minutes to take notes or transcribe the information. It should only be necessary for members to avail themselves of this right to take notes where urgent access to the information in the minutes is required. This is because s 383(3) entitles any member to be furnished with a copy of any such minutes within seven days of making a request to the company for such a copy. The same subsection allows the company to charge a fee for this purpose. This fee is prescribed in Sch 2 of the Companies (Inspection and Copying of Registers, Indexes and Documents) Regulations 1991 as 10p per 100 words or part thereof.[1] The company, and every officer, in default under the section, is liable to a fine (s 383(4)), and the court may make orders for inspection, or direct copies to be sent to the persons requiring them (s 383(5)). These provisions regarding the right to inspect minutes apply equally to minutes embodying written resolutions (s 382A(3)).

There is no requirement that minutes of directors' meetings be available for inspection by members of the company. A director is, by virtue of his or her office, entitled to see minutes of directors' meetings, but, in the absence of an express provision in the articles or an agreement to which the company is a party such as a subscription or shareholders' agreement, shareholders have no such right. The reasoning behind this was expressed in 1859 as follows:

> 'It is highly proper that an inspection of the books containing the proceedings of directors should be obtained on special occasions and for special purposes: but the business of such companies could hardly be conducted if anyone, by buying a share, might entitle himself at all times to gain a knowledge of every commercial transaction to which the directors engage, the moment that an entry of it is made in their books . . . the proposed daily and hourly inspection and publication of all their proceedings . . . would probably ere long be found very prejudicial to shareholders.'[2]

However, the minutes should be accessible to directors and the secretary. Auditors also are entitled under s 389A to see the minutes for the purposes of audit.

In addition, minutes should be kept of committees of the board. These, like minutes of board meetings, should be available for inspection by all the directors, whether or not they were members of the committee. Even if the matter discussed was concerned with a particular director, or affairs in which that director was concerned, and the director was excluded from the committee for that very reason, he or she is entitled as a director to know what decision was taken.

THE MINUTE-BOOKS

As the minutes of general meetings are required to be open for inspection by the members and those of directors' meetings are not, separate books are generally kept for each class of minutes.

---

1   It should be noted that those matters described here as being laid down in the Companies (Inspection and Copying of Registers, Indexes and Documents) Regulations 1991 are, of course, more likely to be subject to change than the provisions of the Act itself.

2   *R v Mariquita Mining Co* (1859) 1 E&E 289.

Section 722 provides that any register, index, minute-book or accounting records required by the Act to be kept by a company may be kept either by making entries in bound books or by recording the matters in question in any other manner, and that where any such register, index, minute-book or books of account is not kept by making entries in a bound book but by some other means, adequate precautions must be taken for guarding against falsification and facilitating its discovery. Ideally, minutes should be kept in a secure place, such as a fireproof safe or other like place. The company and every officer of the company who fails to take adequate precautions are liable to a fine and daily default fines in the case of continued contravention. Consequently, with proper precautions, minutes may now be kept in loose-leaf books.

Section 723 caters for computerised registers and other records. It provides that registers and records can be kept 'otherwise than in a legible form'. However, they must be capable of being reproduced in a legible form. Any reference to inspection or provision of copies of such registers or records in the companies legislation is to be treated as a reference to inspection or copies of the reproduction of the register or record in legible form (s 723(4)).

CONTENTS AND SIGNIFICANCE OF THE MINUTES

(1) General principles

Section 382(2) provides that minutes of any meeting required to be kept by s 382(1) shall be evidence of the proceedings if purporting to be signed by the chairman of that meeting or by the chairman of the next succeeding meeting. Further, by s 382(4), where minutes have been made, in accordance with the provisions of the section, of the proceedings at any general meeting of the company or meeting of directors or managers, the meeting is to be deemed to have been duly held and convened until the contrary is proved, and all proceedings thereat to have duly taken place, and all appointments of directors, managers or liquidators are to be deemed to be valid. It is essential, therefore, that the minutes should contain an accurate record of all proceedings transacted and appointments made (see also Table A, reg 100). This is as true for directors' meetings as for company meetings.

> 'Directors ought to place on record, either in formal minutes or otherwise, the purport and effect of their deliberations and conclusions; and if they do this insufficiently or inaccurately they cannot reasonably complain of inferences different from those which they allege to be right.'[3]

A clear distinction should be carefully drawn between a report and a minute. The former chiefly consists of what was said, the latter consists of what was done or agreed upon, and its place of record is the minutes. Speeches and arguments at a

---

3   *Re Liverpool Household Stores* (1890) 59 LJ Ch at 619.

general meeting may form the material of a newspaper report, but subject to the opening comments of this chapter, the resolution and decisions are the only proper material for the minutes. The minutes will be evidence only of those matters properly entered in them.

Although not required by the Act, minutes are sometimes read or, if previously circulated to the members, taken as read, at the next following meeting, and submitted for verification of their correctness. If regarded as a correct report of the proceedings by those members present at that meeting, they are signed by the chairman. If considered incorrect, they may be modified and then signed. Any discussion on the minutes, except as to their accuracy, is out of order, and the chairman should rule accordingly. Questions arising out of the minutes are permissible with the consent of the meeting if only for information and not for discussion. If there is a conflict of opinion as to their accuracy, an amendment to the motion of their correctness, embodying the suggested alteration, should be put to the meeting and it is obvious that those who were not present at the preceding meeting should not take part in the discussion or vote. The approval of the minutes by a meeting merely verifies their accuracy; it does not necessarily mean that such minutes are adopted or that the resolutions therein have been confirmed or ratified by the subsequent meeting. The person who should sign the minutes in order to ensure that the minutes are evidence of proceedings at the meeting is the chairman of that meeting or the chairman of the succeeding meeting, whether present or not at the previous meeting (s 382(2)). Such a signature places the burden of disproving the accuracy of the minutes upon the person alleging they are inaccurate.

There is no statutory requirement that the minutes be approved by the attendees at the meeting to which they relate, or at the next succeeding meeting, before they are signed by the chair. They can be signed at any time. This is the case even if, being signed by the chair of the succeeding meeting, that person was not the chair of, or even present at, the meeting to which the minutes relate. This means that minutes can still be signed in the event of an emergency, or of a comprehensive change in the members or directors of the directors of the company. However, best practice is for the minutes to be put before the members or directors at the next succeeding meeting before they are signed, if possible.

The signature of the chairman to minutes which embody the terms of a contract may be sufficient to satisfy the Statute of Frauds,[4] where the Statute requires contracts to be evidenced by a memorandum in writing.

Once minutes have been signed, they should not be altered or corrected internally. 'I trust I shall never again see or hear of the secretary of a company, whether under superior directions or otherwise, altering minutes of meetings, either by striking

---

4   *Jones v Victoria Graving Dock* (1877) 2 QBD 314.

out anything or adding anything.'[5] If they are found to be incorrect the proper procedure is to add a further minute or note correcting the mistake, and for the chairman to sign that addition. In this way, anyone who reads them will know the correct position, whereas a minute containing alterations renders it uncertain whether the alterations were authorised. If the original minutes were approved at a later meeting, the addition should also be approved and a record made of it. For similar reasons, pages should not be removed from the minute-book, the pages of which should be numbered consecutively.

The fact that the minutes when duly signed by the chair of the meeting to which the minutes relate, or the next succeeding meeting, are evidence of the proceedings (s 382(2)) casts a burden of proving that the minutes are incorrect upon those so alleging.[6] In order to discharge this burden, evidence may be given to show what in fact was done even if this contradicts the minutes, and evidence may be given of a resolution passed but not recorded in the minutes.[7] Articles sometimes provide that the minutes of a meeting if purporting to be signed by the chairman shall be 'conclusive evidence without any further proof of the facts therein stated'. According to the only reported decision on such an article, evidence cannot be given in such a case to contradict minutes so signed unless it can first be shown that the minutes have been written up fraudulently.[8] There is much doubt whether this decision is correct, and an article so framed is most inadvisable. It would in any case bind only a member of the company, and probably only when dealing with the company in the capacity as such.

The secretary should make the necessary notes as each meeting, whether general or of the board, proceeds, and subsequently write up the minutes in the minute-book. The secretary should take care that the record is absolutely impartial and free from ambiguity, that the exact account of what was actually agreed upon and nothing more is minuted, and that it is sufficiently detailed and complete, so that an absent member would be able to fully understand from the record what was done at the meeting.

The benefits of holding a set of minutes signed by the chairman mean it is undesirable to keep computerised records of minutes without also printing out a hard copy of those minutes and obtaining the signature of the chairman to them.

(2) Board meetings

It is not essential to the validity of the exercise of the power of the directors that their decision should be embodied in formal resolutions, provided that the minutes

5   *Re Cawley & Co* (1889) 42 ChD 209 at 226.
6   *Re Indian Zoedone Co* (1884) 26 ChD 70 at 77.
7   *Re Fireproof Doors* [1916] 2 Ch 142; *Re Pyle Works (No 2)* [1891] 1 Ch 173 at 184.
8   *Kerr v John Mottram Ltd* [1940] Ch 657.

record the substance of the decision made[9] – s 382 applies to board minutes as well as minutes of members' meetings. Nevertheless, the record should be sufficiently clear for absent members of the board to follow the proceedings. The minutes should, therefore, record the names of the directors present. The names of other persons, if recorded, should be stated as being 'in attendance'. In the case of resolutions of directors not carried unanimously, it is desirable to record the names of those who voted for and against the resolution if there is a request for such a record. A director is not entitled to have a protest recorded in the minutes, but if the director votes against a motion he or she is entitled to have that fact noted in the minutes.

As with members' meetings it is generally desirable that the minutes of directors' meetings should not be signed until approved by a subsequent meeting. This is because s 382 provides that minutes of a board meeting, when signed by the chair of the meeting to which they relate, or the chair of the next succeeding meeting are evidence of the proceedings. The burden of proving that the minutes are incorrect is upon those so alleging. If a succeeding meeting of any kind requires the minutes of a previous meeting to be altered before approving them as correct, some reference to this should be made in the minutes of the later meeting. A director who is present at a meeting of the board at which the minutes of a previous board meeting are confirmed, even though that director is a party to their confirmation, is not thereby made responsible for what was resolved upon at such a previous board meeting if the resolution has been acted upon before the minutes are confirmed.[10] Such a director is, however, thereby given notice that such resolution was passed.

Finally, it should be noted that s 382(3) deems a declaration by a shadow director under s 317(8), made through a member of the board, that that shadow director has an interest in a company contract, part of the proceedings at a directors' meeting. Accordingly, such a declaration ought to be noted in the minutes of the meeting.

---

9   *Re Land Credit Co* (1869) LR, 4 Ch App 460 at 473.
10 *Re Lands Allotment Co* [1894] 1 Ch 616 at 635; *Burton v Bevan* [1908] 2 Ch 240.

Chapter 13

SPEECHES AND DEFAMATION

INTRODUCTION

Speeches made at meetings and reports submitted in connection therewith come under the general law relating to defamation. Generally speaking, a person making statements at meetings or in reports has little to fear from the law of defamation provided that person acts with reasonable care, and avoids making unsupportable attacks on character and reputation.

Two basic principles of defamation law should be noted.

(1) A defamatory statement is one which tends to lower a person in the estimation of right-thinking members of society generally,[1] or which tends to make them shun or avoid that person. It does not necessarily have to expose that person to hatred or contempt.[2]

(2) A defamatory statement may be either libel or slander. Libel is in written or some other permanent form whereas slander is in oral or some other transient form. Defamatory statements made on television and radio are libel rather than slander.

DEFENCES GENERALLY

Statements which are at first sight defamatory can often be made with impunity because of the various defences which may be available in libel proceedings.

(1) Justification

The maker of a defamatory statement can plead justification and say that the statement is substantially true and this will generally provide a defence even if the defendant was actuated by malice. It should, however, be noted that the defendant's honest belief that the statement is true is insufficient if he or she cannot prove it is true. Thus, it is a difficult defence to rely upon. However, if a person has

---

1   *Sim v Stretch* [1936] 2 All ER 1237.
2   *Drummond-Jackson v British Medical Association* [1970] 1 WLR 691.

a conviction for a criminal offence, that is proof that he or she has committed that offence.[3]

Section 5 of the Defamation Act 1952 provides that if the defamatory statement contains more than one charge the defence of justification does not fail just because the truth of every charge is not proved, provided the words not proved to be true do not materially injure the plaintiff's reputation having regard to the truth of the remaining charges. *Polly Peck Holdings v Treford*[4] makes a distinction between two situations which may arise under s 5. One situation is where a defamatory statement includes two distinct charges and the other is where the charges are not wholly distinct but have a common sting. In the former situation, if the plaintiff chooses to sue for defamation only in respect of one charge then the defendant cannot bring evidence in respect of the truth of the other charge. However, in the latter situation, the defendant can justify the common sting of the two charges by bringing evidence in respect of the charge of which the plaintiff has not complained.

(2) Fair comment

It is a defence if it can be established that the statement consisted only of fair comment on a matter of public interest. This defence can in turn be defeated by proof that the statement was made maliciously. The following points enlarge upon this defence:

(a) Matters of public interest include, inter alia, the public conduct of everyone taking part in public affairs, the administration of public institutions and local affairs. Normally, the defence is more likely to apply to proceedings of public bodies than to meetings of private bodies such as societies and limited companies, but the conduct of societies and limited companies, whether public or private, can constitute a matter of public interest in some circumstances. Public interest in a matter can arise 'whenever a matter is such as to affect people at large, so that they may be legitimately interested in, or concerned at, what is going on; or what may happen to them or to others'.[5] Thus, a company's conduct towards its employees[6] and the contents of a prospectus issued to the public[7] have been held to be matters of public interest. The defence of fair comment should, it is thought, extend to all prospectuses and any document filed at the Companies Registry for public inspection.

---

3   Civil Evidence Act 1968, s 13.
4   [1986] QB 1000.
5   *London Artists Ltd v Littler* [1969] 2 QB 375.
6   *South Hetton Coal Co v North-Eastern News Association* [1894] 1 QB 133.
7   *Lotinga v Edward Lloyd Ltd* (1910) *The Times*, December 5.

(b) The statement in question must be comment based on true facts and not asserted as fact. The facts upon which the comment is based may be implied from the comment itself or the background to the publication of the comment. Such facts need not be made explicit in the comment.[8] (If a defamatory statement of fact is made, the only defences available are justification or qualified privilege.) It is not necessary to prove the truth of all the allegations of fact provided that the statement is fair comment in the light of those allegations of fact which are proved (Defamation Act 1952, s 6).

(c) The comment must be fair. The test of fairness is not whether a reasonable person would hold the defendant's view but whether the defendant is 'an honest man expressing his genuine opinion on a subject of public interest'.[9] A comment is not fair if it imputes to the person defamed discreditable or improper motives unless a fairminded person may upon those facts have held that opinion.[10]

(d) Malice defeats the defence of fair comment. Malice may be shown in two ways:

(i) *When the person making the statement does so either without honest belief in its truth, or recklessly, that is, is indifferent as to whether the statement is true or false.* It follows that proof of carelessness, negligence, anger, indignation or even of a 'gross and irrational prejudice' will not suffice if the speaker honestly, albeit irrationally, believed what he or she said to be true.[11] But it also follows that repetition of gossip without a belief in its truth is capable of being malicious. Malice in this sense is wider than the commonly understood notion of malice or spite.

(ii) *When the dominant motive of the person making the statement is an improper or extraneous motive, such as spite or private advantage, unconnected with the duty or interest which gives rise to the privilege.* The plaintiff's burden in this case is a heavy one and success is unlikely unless the plaintiff can show either that there was no honest belief in the truth of the statement (in which case malice of the first type is present) or that the maker of the statement realised that it had nothing to do with the interest or duty on which a privilege is based and was merely seizing the opportunity to drag in irrelevant defamatory matter.

(3) Absolute privilege

Privilege may be absolute, in which case it provides a complete defence even where the defendant is actuated by malice. For example, statements made in the

---

8   *Kemsley v Foot* [1952] AC 345.
9   *Slim v Daily Telegraph* [1968] 2 QB 157.
10 *Peter Walker Ltd v Hodgson* [1909] 1 KB 239; *London Artists Ltd v Littler* [1969] 2 QB 375.
11 *Horrocks v Lowe* [1975] AC 135.

Houses of Parliament or in the administration of justice are absolutely privileged. However, in most other cases, privilege is qualified.

(4) Qualified privilege

Where privilege is qualified the statement is protected unless the maker was motivated by malice (see the discussion of malice, above). Qualified privilege may arise under common law or by virtue of statutory provisions.

(a) Common law
Under the common law, qualified privilege applies whenever the person making the statement has an interest, or a legal, social or moral duty to make it to the person to whom it was made, and the person to whom it was made has a corresponding interest or duty to receive it.[12] Reciprocity of interest and duty between the person making the statement and the person to whom it is made is essential.[13] For newspapers to rely on the defence of qualified privilege, they must show that publication is in the public interest and they are fulfilling a duty in publishing.

In respect of qualified privilege, unnecessary publication may be evidence of malice (which destroys the privilege), and the publication may be wider than is justified in the circumstances by the privilege.[14] Thus, where a report has been circulated to members of a committee on a privileged occasion, considered and dealt with, its subsequent re-circulation to the committee may not be the subject of qualified privilege unless it can be shown that it was still reasonably necessary for the performance of the committee's functions or those of its members. This will especially be so if, on the occasion of the first publication, the committee decided to withhold further publication of the report and its membership has, in the meantime, changed so that there is, in effect, a new publication to some of the members.[15]

The presence of the press or other third parties at the making of the defamatory statement does not necessarily prove malice. A distinction should be drawn between the following situations:

(i)   where the press or other third parties happen to be present at a meeting (in accordance with the regular custom of the meeting) where a defamatory statement is made,[16] or if the maker of the statement calls in a third person, such as his or her solicitor, to hear what he or she says as a reasonable

---

12   *Adam v Ward* [1917] AC 309.
13   *Watt v Longsdon* [1930] 1 KB 130.
14   *Cutler v McPhail* [1962] 2 QB 292; *Chapman v Ellesmere* [1932] 2 KB 431.
15   *R v Lancashire County Council Police Authority, ex parte Hook* [1980] QB 603.
16   *Pittard v Oliver* [1891] 1 QB 474.

precaution to protect his or her own interests,[17] in which case the defence of qualified privilege will not be lost;

(ii) where the press or other third parties are expressly invited to attend the meeting by the person making the defamatory statement,[18] in circumstances where it might have been made in private,[19] in which case the defence of qualified privilege may be lost.

If several persons make the defamatory statement at an occasion protected by qualified privilege the defence is lost only by those against whom express malice is proved.[20] The malice of an agent may make a principal liable, but the malice of a principal will not make an innocent agent liable.[21]

(b) Statutory provisions

Different types of qualified privilege exist under the Defamation Act 1952. For example, qualified privilege attaches to reports of Parliamentary and judicial proceedings. Of particular interest in this context is the qualified privilege which attaches to the publication in a newspaper or broadcast of matters occurring in meetings of specified bodies. However, this privilege will not protect a defendant where there is publication of any matter which is prohibited by law or is not in the public interest.[22]

The publication of statements made in the meetings of some of these bodies are privileged without explanation or contradiction. For others, explanation or contradiction is necessary if requested by the plaintiff.[23] This work is primarily concerned with the latter class of bodies. These bodies include local authorities, commissions of enquiry, lawful public meetings and general meetings of public companies. General meetings of private companies are not included, and defendants must rely on the common law defences of justification or fair comment in respect of any defamatory reports of such meetings.

The Defamation Act 1996 extended the specific privilege attaching to the reports of public bodies so that it applies to any publication, not just publication in newspapers or broadcasts, although reports must be fair and accurate for the privilege to apply.

---

17 *Taylor v Hawkins* (1851) 16 QB 308.
18 *Pittard v Oliver* [1891] 1 QB 474.
19 *Toogood v Spyring* (1834) 1 Cr M&R 181.
20 *Longdon-Griffiths v Smith* [1951] 1 KB 295.
21 *Eggar v Viscount Chelmsford* [1965] 1 QB 248.
22 Defamation Act 1952, s 7(3).
23 Ibid, s 7(2); *Khan v Ahmed* [1957] 2 QB 149.

(5) Innocent dissemination

It is now, under the Defamation Act 1996, a defence for the defendant to show that he was not the author, editor or publisher of the statement complained of, and that he did not know, having taken reasonable care, that he was publishing a defamatory statement. In this context the publisher is used to mean commercial publisher in the broadest sense. For example, printers do not fall within that category and so are given protection by this section. However, the most important qualification is the requirement to have taken reasonable care. If the defendant had any reason to suppose that the statement might be defamatory he should have made further enquiries.

COMPANIES

In most cases, statements made in a company meeting, in a board meeting and in reports and circulars to the shareholders are protected by qualified privilege. Evidence of malice destroys the privilege.

(1) Meetings

Qualified privilege protects persons making statements in good faith in a company meeting on a subject in which the members are interested, that is, where the person making the statement has an interest or a legal, social or moral duty to make it to the members, and the members have a corresponding duty or interest to receive it; the privilege may be lost if the statement is made privately after the determination of the meeting instead of as part of the proceedings.[24] Statements about the auditors, particular employees, or the directors are examples of subjects in which the members are interested.

The general rule as to the presence of outsiders, stated above, applies so that, provided the person making the defamatory statement has not sought the presence of the press or other third parties at the meeting, the privilege is not destroyed merely through their presence.

(2) Reports and circulars

Reports and circulars sent to the members of the company by the company[25] or by some other members[26] are privileged in the absence of malice. In order to ensure that malice will be regarded as absent, those drafting reports and circulars must ensure that they have an honest belief in the truth of the contents and that there is no unnecessary publication ie they must take care to ensure that the reports and

---

24   *Martin v Strong* (1836) 5 A&E 535.
25   *Lawless v Anglo-Egyptian Cotton Co* (1869) LR 4 QB 262.
26   *Quartz Hill Gold Mining Co v Beall* (1882) 20 ChD 501.

circulars only reach the intended recipient and are not, for example, capable of being opened and read by someone else.

(3) Board meetings

Directors of a company have a duty to discuss the affairs of their company and they are entitled to discuss the conduct of their officials so long as they do so honestly.[27] Statements about the company's business made by a director to an official or a member of the company or to the company's solicitor are normally privileged.[28] An example of the way in which this privilege may be lost by unnecessary publication occurred in *Watt v Longsdon*.[29] In this case, it was held that the defendant director was under a duty to communicate to his chairman a letter of complaint about the conduct of the plaintiff employee, but that he was under no duty to communicate the contents of the letter to the plaintiff's wife. Communication to the plaintiff's wife, therefore, destroyed the privilege.

PARTIES

There is a distinction between defaming a corporation and defaming its officers.

(1) Companies generally

A company cannot commence proceedings for words which reflect not upon the company but solely upon its individual officers or members.[30] Further, a trading company may only sue for defamation to protect its trading character.[31]

The trading character of a company may be injured by statements made at meetings or in reports. Thus, it may be defamatory to make a statement reflecting on the conduct of a company's trade[32] or on its financial stability.[33]

A company can sue one of its own directors or members for defamation.[34]

(2) Non-trading companies

Non-trading companies are only entitled to sue for defamation if they are not 'governing bodies'. This principle was laid down by the House of Lords in

---

27 *Allan v Clarke* (1912) *The Times*, January 17.
28 *M'Gillivray v Davidson* (1934) SLT 45.
29 [1930] 1 KB 130.
30 See, further, Patfield 'Protecting the Reputation of Corporate Personnel, Organs and Associates' (1988) 18 *University of Western Australia Law Review* 203.
31 *South Hetton Coal Co v North-Eastern News Association Ltd* [1893] 1 QB 133.
32 *D and L Caterers Ltd and Jackson v d'Anjou* [1945] KB 364.
33 *Irish People's Assurance Society v City of Dublin Assurance Co Ltd* (1929) IR 25.
34 *Metropolitan Saloon v Hawkins* (1859) 4 H&N 87.

Derbyshire County Council v Times Newspapers Ltd, in which a municipal corporation was prevented from pursuing a defamation action on this basis.[35] Governing corporations may therefore only sue where the statement amounts to a malicious falsehood, in relation to which proof of malice is (of course) necessary.[36]

It appears that most non-governing non-trading companies are entitled to sue for defamation, although only where, as with trading companies, the words reflect on the activity of the company rather than merely the individuals who compose it.[37]

The decision in *Derbyshire County Council v Times Newspapers Ltd* was based to some extent on a common law principle of freedom of expression. The European Convention of Human Rights has now been incorporated into UK law although, at the date of publication it is not clear when it will come into force. The Convention provides that Article 10, the right to freedom of expression, may mean that the principle in *Derbyshire County Council v Times Newspapers Ltd* may be extended to other bodies.

---

35 [1993] 2 WLR 449. See, further, Patfield 'Corporate Public Authorities and Freedom of
    Speech' (1993) 14 *The Company Lawyer* 98.
36 *Ratcliffe v Evans* [1892] 2 QB 524.
37 *Saskatchewan College of Physicians and Surgeons v Co-operative Commonwealth Federation
    Publishing and Printing Co Ltd* (1951) 51 DLR (2d) 442.

Chapter 14

ADMISSION TO AND EXPULSION FROM MEMBERS' AND DIRECTORS' MEETINGS

ADMISSION TO MEETINGS (INCLUDING THE PRESS)

One of the matters which must sometimes be decided in connection with meetings is who should be invited to attend. Generally speaking, in the case of private meetings such as a meeting of members or directors of a company, there is no right to attend for the public or press, but the meeting itself may decide whether outsiders of any kind shall be permitted to be present. Large public companies, for example, generally desire that their general meetings shall be reported in the papers, and so invite the attendance of reporters, but they are not bound to do so.

When a meeting of a company takes place in premises which are private property or to which a stranger has no right of access,[1] a stranger may only remain so long as no objection is made to his or her presence. If the stranger is requested to leave and refuses to do so then he or she becomes a trespasser and may be ejected with such reasonable force as is required. It is unnecessary for these purposes that any reason be given to support the request that the stranger leave.

The expulsion, however, of a person who is entitled to attend a meeting (except for disorderly conduct of a serious nature) is illegal unless the articles or operating procedures (if any) of the company provide otherwise.

> 'The power, therefore, of suspending a member guilty of obstruction or disorderly conduct during the continuance of any current sitting, is . . . reasonably necessary for the proper exercise of the functions of any legislative assembly of this kind; and it may very well be, that the same doctrine of reasonable necessity would authorise a suspension until submission or apology by the offending member; which, if he were refractory, might cause it to be prolonged (not by the arbitrary discretion of the assembly, but by his own wilful default) for some further time.'[2]

Similarly, in *Doyle v Falconer*,[3] it was said that if a member of a colonial House of Assembly was guilty of disorderly conduct in that House while sitting, he might be removed or excluded for a time or even expelled, and that if the conduct of the

---

1   It is an offence to use or threaten violence to secure entry into any premises.
2   *Barton v Taylor* (1886) 11 App Cas 197, at 204; a case concerned with the New South Wales Assembly.
3   LR 1 PC 328 at 340.

members was not such as to secure order and decency of debate, the law would sanction the use of that degree of force which might be necessary to remove the person offending from the place of meeting and to keep him excluded, and that the same rule would apply even more so to obstructions caused by a non-member. In either case, if the violation of order amounted to a breach of the peace, recourse might be had to the ordinary courts.

It is the duty of the chairman to preserve order at the meeting, and consequently, in the event of a person otherwise entitled to attend a meeting being so disorderly as to interfere unduly with the reasonable conduct of the meeting or to prevent the proper transaction of business, the chairman may order that person to withdraw. If the person concerned refuses to comply with this order, he or she may be ejected with reasonable force. If the disorderly person resists ejection, this may constitute a breach of the peace. It is usually desirable, however, that the chairman should be supported by the majority of the meeting before ordering a person to withdraw, and should take care not to give instructions for ejection unless he or she is quite sure such instructions will be expeditiously and efficiently carried out.

If it is anticipated in advance of a proposed general meeting of members of the company that the meeting will be 'so disrupted by a minority that no orderly business can be conducted' an application can be made to the court under s 371. The court can make an order which will enable the meeting to be called and held in such a way as to avoid the anticipated disruption. The order made can even override the company's articles of association.[4]

---

4   *Re British Union for the Abolition of Vivisection* (1995) *The Times*, March 3.

Chapter 15

MEETINGS AND ELECTRONIC COMMUNICATIONS

This chapter addresses two questions. First, can notice of a meeting be given by electronic communication? Secondly, can meetings be held electronically? Possible ways to give notice of a meeting electronically are telephone, videoconferencing, e-mail, fax or posting of the notice on a website. Possible ways to hold a meeting electronically are telephone, videoconferencing and e-mail.

It must begin, though, with words of caution. First, there has been virtually no recognition of technological advances in the company legislation or common law of the UK. This means that none of the practices discussed below have a statutory authority or have been tested in the courts. Indeed, certain of them, even those already in use by companies, should be adopted only after specific, specialist advice has been taken. Where such advice is recommended this is flagged in the discussion. Secondly, the Government unveiled plans to introduce legislation to facilitate e-commerce in late 1998. This is likely to address such issues such as legal validity of digital signatures, which will impact on the law in relation to company meetings. Those interested in this area should monitor the progress of this potential new legislation carefully since it may supersede what is written below.

ELECTRONIC NOTICE OF DIRECTORS' MEETINGS

Notice of a directors' meeting can be given electronically provided the articles of the company do not specifically prohibit it, and (in accordance with existing case-law on the giving of notice) provided it is reasonable to do so. The author's view is that Table A does not prohibit electronic notices. Giving notice of directors' meetings electronically will probably be considered reasonable if all the directors are likely to become aware of the meeting by virtue of the electronic communication.

To avoid disputes the directors may wish to agree and minute guidelines to regulate the calling of their meetings electronically. For example, they may agree that each director should provide a specific telephone or fax number, or an e-mail address, for the purposes of giving notice. Notice is properly given only if the sender rings or faxes that number or e-mails that address.

In the case of a telephone call, the guidelines might provide that the telephone must be answered and the notice relayed to the director personally. Alternatively, it might be agreed as sufficient to record the content of the notice on an answering machine or voicemail.

In any event, it is strongly recommended that notice of board meetings should only be given electronically if the directors have unanimously agreed to this, and any specific guidelines to be adopted.

It would be technologically possible to give notice by posting it on a website 'bulletin board'. This is not specifically prohibited by the companies legislation, but legally it would be novel. A company would need specific, specialist advice before adopting this practice. The author is not aware of any company that has actually taken this step.

In the case of faxes and e-mails the guidelines might require the sender to check for confirmation that the electronic message has been received by the receiving fax machine or has arrived in the relevant e-mailbox.

Unauthorised access can be gained to electronic communications over the Internet – e-mail messages. They can be 'hacked'. For reasons which often have no basis in fact the public perception is that this danger is greater on the Internet than over, say, a telephone system. The directors may therefore wish to consider security issues if notices are to be given using e-mail.

The security of Internet communications are beyond the remit of this book, but there are means of restricting access to e-mails using passwords allocated only to particular users, by creating an intranet or extranet using 'firewalls' or by using encryption techniques. The board may wish to consult their IT departments or buy in outside IT expertise to deal with this issue.

HOLDING DIRECTORS' MEETINGS ELECTRONICALLY

It is increasingly common for directors' meetings to be held electronically. However, a number of practical issues need to be resolved if this is not to cause problems. It is sensible for decisions on these issues to be included in the company's articles of association. Table A makes no provision for electronic meetings but modern articles of association will do so. See Appendix for a precedent.

The articles should define the conditions necessary to hold a valid electronic meeting. The overriding requirement will usually be that the means of electronic communication enables each director to hear and be heard by the other participants. This means there can be a debate or exchange leading to a resolution in the best interests of the company, as there would be at a conventional meeting.

Electronic board meetings commonly take the form of a telephone or videoconferencing link. It would be technologically possible to link directors by e-mail or set up an electronic bulletin board on a website. Such Internet-based means of communication would allow directors to see and contribute to a written debate in real time. The practical difference between these Internet-based means of exchange and exchanges where the participants actually speak to each other is that participants using the former cannot interrupt each other. This may be considered beneficial in some companies. However, the author's view is that this would create legal uncertainties, particularly in relation to verification of the identities of the participants. In practice, the author is not aware of board meetings being held electronically other than via telephone or videoconferencing.

An important issue is to decide where the electronic board meeting is being held. In a conventional meeting all the directors are gathered in one place. The meeting is clearly held in that place. However, if directors communicating electronically are in different places, where is the meeting held?

This could cause tax problems if, for example, a director or, more likely, a majority of the directors regularly participate in electronic board meetings from a jurisdiction which taxes companies, wherever incorporated, whose central management and control is located there. If the fiscal authorities learn that directors on their territory participate electronically in board meetings of a UK company they may investigate further.

Where central management and control is exercised will be a question of fact under the law of the jurisdiction concerned. However, the articles of association may be persuasive under that law. It may, therefore, be important that they prescribe where the company considers the meeting is being held, or the basis upon which that question should be resolved so the local tax authority can be referred to them. For example, it is common for articles to say the meeting is deemed held where the chair is physically present or, alternatively, where the directors agree.

Alternatively, the articles could avoid this problem altogether by prohibiting electronic meetings if a director or majority of the directors participating are physically present outside the UK. Such directors would either have to travel to the UK, forego their right to attend the meeting or, if authorised by the articles, appoint an alternate director in accordance with any rules in this respect in the articles. But the tax problem would be avoided.

These problems can also arise in more conventional situations. For example, where is the decision made if directors, physically present in a number of different jurisdictions, all sign an unanimous resolution in writing in lieu of a meeting? They are not, therefore, issues only concerning electronic meetings. It is just that they need to be addressed if the benefits of electronic meetings are to be fully enjoyed without legal mishaps.

If security is a concern in relation to electronic notices of meetings, it will be even more so in relation to the confidential matters debated at an electronic board meeting. Again, appropriate IT advice may be required.

ELECTRONIC NOTICE OF GENERAL MEETINGS

Relevant parts of the companies legislation and Table A appear to be based upon a presumption that notice of general meetings will be in hard copy form. For example, s 369 of the Act (though it is primarily concerned with the length of notice to be given in the case of general meetings) consistently uses the term 'notice in writing'. However it is possible to construe this wording in a way which will cover the giving of notice electronically. There are a number of companies whose articles permit the giving of notice of general meetings by fax or e-mail. It is prudent in such articles to build in safeguards which protect members. For example, they will often provide that notice can only be sent to a member electronically if the member concerned has consented in writing, provided a relevant fax number or e-mail address, and the electronic means used enables the member to read the text of the message (which will not necessarily be the case in every instance). The articles should also regulate when notice given electronically is deemed to have been issued.

What of a notice of a general meeting given to the holder of a share warrant to bearer? One consequence of the issue of share warrants to bearer is that the name of the holder of the shares is struck out of the register of members (s 355 of the Act). Subsequently, the ownership of the shares comprised in the warrant can be transferred to a new holder or 'bearer' by delivery of the warrant, without reference to the company. This means that the company has no means of knowing who the bearer is when it calls general meetings. Clearly it cannot give notice to warrant holders in the same way as it does to registered holders.

The practice is for the articles which authorise the company to issue warrants to bearer either to include specific alternative means of giving notice or to provide that the directors may specify such alternatives when issuing the warrants. Often these conditions are printed on the back of the warrant.

The usual provision is for notice of the general meeting to be given to warrant holders by advertising the notice in some predetermined publications such as national newspapers. In time, if Internet access becomes as common as purchase of a newspaper, there seems no reason why the rules could not provide that this notice can be given by posting it on the company's website either in addition or as an alternative to a newspaper advertisement. However, there is as yet, no statutory or other authority for this proposition under current law.

HOLDING MEMBERS' MEETINGS ELECTRONICALLY

The law governing holding of members' meetings is redolent with the presumption that a physical meeting will actually be held. It is extremely difficult to construe many of the relevant provisions of the companies legislation in a way which would justify the holding of members' meetings electronically.

For example, para 29 Part IV of Sch 13 of the Act requires that a copy of the register of directors' interests in shares and debentures should be available for inspection at every annual general meeting. This appears to preclude the annual general meeting being held electronically.

Sections 95(5), 157(4)(a), 164(6) and (7), 174(4), 319(5) and 337(3)(a) require physical documents and/or statements to be present at general meetings if convened to consider certain matters. This appears to preclude the holding of electronic meetings to consider these matters (although Sch 15A of the Act does provide specific alternative procedures which permit such matters to be decided by statutory resolution in writing under ss 381A to 381C of the Act).

A company holding a members' meeting electronically would need new ways to check the bona fides of a participant purporting to be a proxy, or a representative of a corporate member under s 375 of the Act. The procedures for voting on a poll could be difficult to manage.

Whilst it may be possible to deal with these points on an item by item basis, their cumulative effect is to create a formidable concern around the idea of purporting to hold a members' meeting electronically. The only circumstance in which such a meeting might be envisaged would be if the electronic means used were videoconferencing *and* if all members participated.

The authority for suggesting the use of videoconferencing is that this was used in the London Life[1] case. London Life gave notice of an annual general meeting for a venue which turned out to be too small to accommodate those who turned up. A hasty switch of venues was arranged. The new arrangements included use of certain outer rooms which were connected to the main hall by a video-conferencing facility. Whilst the issues for decision did not include the validity of videoconferencing, the court appeared to find nothing objectionable in its use.

On one construction this was a meeting held by videoconference. It was just that one set of participants – those in the main room in the venue – was very much larger than the others. However, this was not argued in court and the preferable construction must be that there was an actual physical meeting. The videoconferencing facilities were merely to ensure everyone could take part, similar to the way microphones are commonly used to make sure everyone can hear what is being said. Certainly, the meeting was convened in the usual way.

---

1   *Byng v London Life Association Ltd* [1989] BCLC 400.

The authority for suggesting that unanimity might make the electronic meeting valid is, of course, the line of cases which includes *Cane v Jones*, referred to at page 20. However, if there is unanimity among the members decisions can equally be dealt with by all members agreeing (electronically) a form of words for written resolution in writing in lieu of a meeting which they could then all prepare and sign (whilst remaining in electronic communication if they wish) in accordance with well-established law. However, the better view must be that electronic members' meetings are not permitted under current law, even if held by videoconference and with the unanimous participation of the members.

Chapter 16

MEETINGS IN INSOLVENCY

INTRODUCTION

This Part has so far been concerned with meetings held in relation to the affairs of the company while it is a going concern and not directly threatened with proceedings in respect of insolvency. In this chapter, provisions dealing with the main meetings required to be held in connection with the insolvency of companies are noted. The central statutory provisions in this area are drawn from the Insolvency Act 1986 (IA 1986). The Insolvency Rules 1986, SI 1986/1925, (the Rules) also have an important role to play.[1] Invaluable practical guidance on the conduct of certain types of insolvency meetings can be found in the Statements of Insolvency Practice (SIP) issued from time to time by the Council of the Society of Practitioners of Insolvency.[2]

COMPANY VOLUNTARY ARRANGEMENTS

(1) Meetings to be held

The Act and the Rules make a distinction between company voluntary arrangements in two circumstances relevant to the issue of meetings. The first of these two circumstances is where the arrangement is proposed by the directors to the company and its creditors at a time when the company is not in administration and is not being wound up (IA 1986, s 1(1)). The second is where the proposal is made by the administrator or the liquidator (IA 1986, s 1(3)). There are some differences in the provisions relating to the required meetings in these two cases, which are explored below. There is also much common ground between the two types of

---

1   References to Rules in this chapter will be to the Insolvency Rules 1986. For Scotland, reference should be made to the provisions governing procedure in Scotland and the Insolvency (Scotland) Rules 1986, SI 1986/1915, as amended.

2   The statements of insolvency practice are for the purpose of guidance to insolvency practitioners and may not be relied upon as having any legal effect or as definitive statements. Of general importance is SIP 12 which requires that the responsible insolvency practitioner should always create a record of the meeting which should be prepared in accordance with the provisions there set out.

company voluntary agreements. Both, for example, require a nominee[3] who is a qualified insolvency practitioner in relation to the company to supervise the implementation of any arrangement agreed upon. Where the nominee is not the administrator or liquidator then meetings of members and creditors may be required if the nominee considers it necessary (IA 1986, s 2(2)). Where the nominee is the administrator or liquidator then meetings of members and creditors are obligatory (IA 1986, s 3(2)). The purpose of the meetings in both cases is to consider the proposals for the company voluntary arrangement and decide whether to agree to them, or to agree to them in some amended form. Neither meeting has an absolutely unfettered right to agree to any proposal (see the limitations in IA 1986, s 4(3) and (4) and s 6), but once held, the agreement of the meeting is essential for any proposal to go ahead.

(2) Notice

(a) Nominee is not administrator or liquidator
Where the nominee is not the administrator or liquidator, but has reported to the court under IA 1986, s 2(2) that the meetings should be held, then the nominee should, unless the court directs otherwise, summon the meetings for the time and place proposed in the report (IA 1986, s 3(1)). The date of the meeting should be not less than 14, nor more than 28 days after the filing of the report in the court (r 1.9(1)) and at least 14 days' notice should be given (r 1.9(2)). This minimum notice period of 14 days excludes the day of sending the notice and the day of the meeting. Although the Rules require 'receipt' of the notice by the creditor, r 12.10 treats such notice as being received on the second or fourth day after posting (depending on whether it was sent by first or second class post) unless the contrary is proved by the 'recipient'.[4] So long as the requisite documents are sent to a creditor and that creditor in fact becomes aware of the meeting before it takes place, the strict requirement of the Rules as to notice will be complied with.[5] It has also been held that creditors should be entitled to attend and vote at a meeting of which they had actual notice, regardless of whether they were given notice of it by the nominee or in accordance with the Rules.[6]

So far as the creditors' meeting is concerned, notice must be given to all creditors specified in the statement of affairs and any other creditors, the name and address

---

3   For the duties of the nominee to test the proposal see *Re Greystoke v Hamilton-Smith* [1997] BPIR 24 (a case concerning individual voluntary arrangements). Best practice is set out generally in SIP 3.
4   *Skipton Building Society v Collins* [1998] BPIR 267.
5   *Beverley Group plc v McClue* [1996] BPIR 25.
6   *Re Debtors (Nos 400 IO and 401 IO of 1996)* [1997] BPIR 431.

of whom the nominee is aware (IA 1986, s 3(3); see also r 1.9(2)(a)).[7] So far as the members' meeting is concerned, notice must be sent to all persons who are, according to the nominee's belief, members (r 1.9(2)(b)). Fourteen days' notice of both meetings should also be given to the directors and officers and any person who the convenor considers should be present because that person was a director or officer of the company during the two years immediately preceding the notice (r 1.16(1)).

For both creditors' and members' meetings the notice should, of course, stipulate the time and place of the meeting. The time of the meeting must be fixed for between 10.00 am and 4.00 pm on a business day (r 1.13(2)), and although both the members' and creditors' meetings should be held on the same day and at the same place, the creditors' meeting must be held before the members' meeting (r 1.13(3)). This reflection of the status accorded to creditors in a company voluntary arrangement is also shown by the fact that in fixing the venue, the convenience of the creditors should be accorded primary regard (r 1.13(1)).

Certain other matters are also required to be stated in the notice. These are laid down in r 1.9(3) and include a specification of the court to which the nominee's report has been delivered; a statement of the rules on requisite majorities; a copy of the proposal; a copy or summary of the statement of affairs; and the nominee's comments on the proposal. The notice must also be accompanied by a proxy form (r 1.13(4)). No proxy form shall be pre-completed by the insertion in it of the name or description of any person (ie for appointment as an insolvency office holder or for appointment as a member of a committee or as proxy holder) (r 8.2).[8]

(b) Nominee is administrator or liquidator
Where the nominee is the administrator or liquidator then the nominee should summon the meeting for the time and place he or she thinks fit (IA 1986, s 3(3)). At least 14 days' notice must be given of the meetings (r 1.11(1)). The creditors, members, directors, officers, former directors and former officers to whom notice should be sent are the same as those identified above in relation to a company voluntary agreement where the company is not in administration or liquidation (see IA 1986, s 3(3) and r 1.11). The provisions on the fixing of time and place of the meeting are also the same (r 1.13). In addition to stating the time and place of the relevant meeting, the notice must also state the effect of the rules on requisite majorities, include a copy of the insolvency practitioner's proposal, and include a copy or summary of the statement of affairs (r 1.11(2)). The notice must be

---

7   By giving notice of the meeting to a creditor, the nominee is acknowledging his status as a creditor for the purpose of the meeting. For this reason, the inclusion of a creditor in the statement of affairs can have important procedural consequences both for the creditor and the company/debtor, see, eg *Re Debtors (Nos 400 IO and 401 IO of 1996)* [1997] BPIR 431 and *Re Bielecki* [1998] BPIR 655.
8   See SIP 10.

accompanied by a proxy form (r 1.13(4)). No proxy form shall be pre-completed by the insertion in it of the name or description of any person (ie for appointment as an insolvency office holder or for appointment as a member of a committee or as proxy holder) (r 8.2).[9]

(3) Chairman[10]

The convenor of the meeting is also to be the chairman of the meeting (r 1.14(1)). After the chairman has presented his report to the creditors' meeting he should allow creditors an opportunity to make comments, ask questions or propose modifications to the proposal. Although it is not a statutory requirement for directors to consent to modifications, SIP 3 recommends that the nominee should find out and report to the meeting the views of the directors on any proposed modifications which they may be required to implement if approved. The creditors' meeting has the power to modify any of the terms of the proposal, including those as to remuneration of the insolvency practitioners.[11] If, however, the convenor is for some reason unable to attend the meeting, the convenor may nominate as chairman a person qualified as an insolvency practitioner in relation to the company, or an employee of the convenor or the convenor's firm experienced in insolvency matters. The Rules lay down a number of powers to be enjoyed by the chairman in addition to the chairman's usual power to regulate the meeting. The chairman may exclude any director, officer, former director or former officer from attending all or part of a meeting, even where that person has been sent a notice of the meeting (r 1.16(2)). The chairman also has a discretion to reject the whole or part of a creditor's claim to be entitled to vote (r 1.17(4)),[12] although if the chairman is in doubt as to the validity of the claim he or she may mark the claim as objected to but allow the creditor to vote (r 1.17(6)).[13] The decision of a chairman to reject the claim to vote of a creditor is subject to appeal to the court by a member or creditor (r 1.17(5)),[14] but any appeal must be made within 28 days from the day that the report on the meetings under IA 1986, s 4(6) has been made to the court (r 1.17(8)). On such an appeal, it is likely that the court will not be limited to consideration of the evidence which was before the chairman, but will come to a conclusion on all the evidence subsequently filed at court whether on balance a

---

9   See SIP 10.
10 For a recent review of the case-law relating to the powers and duties of a chairman of a meeting see *Link Agricultural Pty Ltd v Shanahan* (1998) 28 ACSR 498. See also *Re Chevron Furnishers Pty Ltd* (1992) 8 ACSR 726.
11 See para 2.5.2 of SIP 9 'Remuneration of insolvency office holders'.
12 In an extreme case, it might be appropriate for the chairman to disallow votes which have been cast in order to gain a collateral advantage (eg a competitor aiming for the collapse of the business) and not in the interest of the unsecured creditors as a class, see *Re Laserworks Computer Services Inc* (1997) 48 CBR (3d) 8.
13 See *Re A Debtor (No 222 of 1990)* [1992] BCLC 137.
14 As to which see *Re Sweatfield* [1998] BPIR 276.

creditor's proof should be admitted in whole or in part for voting purposes.[15] Particular powers of the chairman in relation to creditors' meetings are conferred by r 1.19(5). This sub-rule confers on the chairman power to decide whether creditors' votes ought to be left out of account because they are secured in some way, and also power to decide whose votes should be discounted on the basis that they are a connected person (these matters are discussed further below). These powers conferred by r 1.19(5) should be exercised by the chairman in reliance upon the company's statement of affairs.

There is a limitation on the chairman's power when exercising proxy votes. Essentially, unless specifically directed to do so by the appointor, the chairman cannot use proxies to change the amount of remuneration and expenses of the nominee or any supervisor of the proposed arrangement (r 1.15).

(4) Proxies

The courts are increasingly flexible when interpreting the Act and Rules to decide whether proxies are valid and proxy holders are entitled to vote, and it is likely that a proxy holder is entitled to vote provided the proxies are lodged before the vote is taken even if not presented before the meeting started.[16] A faxed proxy is valid for the purposes of the insolvency legislation.[17] If modifications are proposed by a creditor the chairman should give careful consideration to the manner in which he will use specific instructions given to him by creditors to vote for either the acceptance or the rejection of the original proposal. If the words in the proxy form allowing the exercise of discretion in the absence of specific instructions have not been deleted so as to entitle the proxy holder to vote only as directed, the proxy holder is entitled to vote or abstain on any proposed modification at his discretion.[18] However, the chairman should consider most carefully the impact of the exercise of his discretion upon expressed intentions of any creditor who has completed a proxy requiring a vote on any particular resolution. He should bear in mind that, if a creditor is aggrieved that a vote on proposed modifications has taken place and a decision reached which might have been different if creditors represented by proxy had been present at the meeting or had been given the opportunity of amending their proxy, the aggrieved creditor may subsequently challenge the decision (see below). The chairman should consider an adjournment to give him time to explain the position to the creditors from whom he holds proxies and to obtain further instructions.[19] Rules 8.1 to 8.7 deal with representation of a creditor by proxy. All proxies used must be retained by the chairman and delivered to the responsible insolvency practitioner forthwith after the meeting who must, so long as they are in

---

15 *Re A Company (No 004539 of 1993)* [1995] BCC 116 at 120(F–G).
16 *Re Philip Alexander Securities & Futures Ltd* [1998] BPIR 383.
17 *Commissioners of Inland Revenue v Conbeer and White* [1996] BPIR 398.
18 See para 7.8 of SIP 3.
19 See para 7.9 of SIP 3.

his hands, allow them to be inspected by the creditors at all reasonable times, on any business day (rr 8.4 and 8.5)).

(5) Adjournment

The provisions on adjournment of the meetings convened for the purpose of approving a company voluntary arrangement are contained in r 1.21. Not only does the chairman have power to adjourn the meetings, but if the chairman thinks fit, he or she may procure the holding of the creditors' and members' meeting together (r 1.21(1)). Neither the creditors' meeting nor the members' meeting may be adjourned unless the other is also adjourned to the same business day (r 1.21(4)).

The chairman's power of adjournment may only be exercised for the purpose of achieving the requisite majority for the approval of the proposed arrangement (r 1.21(2)). However, even where the meetings are adjourned several times, the final meetings must take place within 14 days of the day originally set down for the holding of the meetings (r 1.21(3)).

The chairman's power to adjourn may be exercised without a resolution of the meeting, but where such a resolution is passed the chairman must adjourn the meeting (r 1.21(2)). Where the proposal for the company voluntary arrangement has been made by the directors and the meeting has been adjourned the nominee must immediately give notice of that fact to the court (r 1.21(5)).

(6) Voting

(a) Creditors' meeting
Every creditor given notice of the meeting is entitled to vote (r 1.17(1)). The issue of creditors' voting rights has given rise to the greatest difficulty. This is partly explained by the potentially serious adjustment of a creditors' rights which occurs when an arrangement is approved. Every creditor who in accordance with the rules had notice of and was entitled to vote at the meeting is bound by the arrangement if it is approved whether or not that creditor actually attended and voted (s 5(2)(b)).[20] In that event, his debt will usually be released or suspended and replaced by the bundle of rights set out in the arrangement. With so much at stake, the chairman also has a difficult task. It is incumbent on a creditor who wishes to vote in respect of his debt to state to the best of his ability the total amount that is owing to him, and if the value of his debt or some part of it is not ascertained to state that fact, and to supply the chairman with as much information as is available to enable the

---

20   For an analysis of the effect of approval of an arrangement on creditors and third parties such as *Johnson v Davies* [1998] 2 All ER 649. As to whether a creditor served with notice of the meeting in respect of one debt will be bound if the proposals are approved in respect of other debts, see *Re Bradley-Hole* [1995] BCC 418 and *Re K G Hoare* [1997] BPIR 683.

chairman to put an estimated value upon it. It does not lie in the mouth of a creditor who remains silent to say subsequently that he is not bound in respect of a claim which he has not mentioned.[21] The calculation of a creditor's voting power is made according to the quantum of the creditor's debt at the date of the meeting, or, where the company is in administration or liquidation, at the date of the administration or liquidation order (r 1.17(2)). Unless the chairman agrees to an estimated value, there is no right to vote in respect of an unliquidated debt or a debt for an unascertained amount (r 1.17(3)). This provision has caused considerable recourse to the courts.[22] Certain parts of debt for an ascertained amount are also to be discounted in the voting process. The discounted interests are laid down in r 1.19(3), which basically excludes amounts of the debt which are in any way secured and debts in respect of which written notice has not been given to the chairman. Secured creditors can vote but their secured claim will be left out of account[23] such that they will become bound by the approval of the arrangement even though their votes will only have been counted to the extent that they are unsecured and, if unascertained, agreed by the chairman. A creditor with security over the company's assets must proceed with care in case he should be taken by his conduct in voting to have surrendered his security.[24] The rights of the secured creditors to enforce their security must not be affected by the arrangement as approved except with their consent (s 4(3)).

The required majority in the creditors' meeting for approval or modification of the proposed arrangement is three-quarters by value (r 1.19(1)). For any other resolution the required majority is one half (r 1.19(2)). However, these required majorities are subject to the rule that any resolution will be invalid if half of the value of valid votes are cast against it, unless that half includes persons connected with the company (r 1.19(4)).

The proposal is deemed to have been rejected if both the creditors' and members' meetings fail to approve it, or a modified version of it, at or before a final adjourned meeting (r 1.21(6)).

---

21 *Re K G Hoare* [1997] BPIR 683.
22 See the review of the cases concerning both individual and company voluntary arrangements in Stephen A Lawson *Individual Voluntary Arrangements*, 2nd edn (Jordans, 1996) at para 6.1.15(3). It is now clear from the decision of the Court of Appeal in *Doorbar v Alltime Securities Ltd* [1996] 1 WLR 456, that it is sufficient if the chairman expresses his willingness to put, and puts, an estimated minimum value on the debt. There is no need for an 'agreement' with the creditor.
23 *Calor Gas Ltd v Piercy* [1994] BCC 69.
24 *Moor v Anglo-Italian Bank* (1879) 10 ChD 681; *Seventeenth Canute Pty Ltd v Bradley Air Conditioning Pty Ltd* (1986) 11 ACLC 193; *Andrew v FarmStart* (1988) 71 CBR (NS) 124; 54 DLR (4th) 406; and *Health & Life Care v SA Asset Mgt* (1995) 18 ACSR 153.

(b) Members' meeting

Calculation of members' voting rights is considerably more straightforward than those of creditors. Members' voting rights are simply as defined in the articles (r 1.18(1)). This is subject to one qualification, which is that members with no voting rights under the articles may vote (r 1.18(2)). The exercise of such a vote, however, seems largely symbolic. This is because such votes are discounted when calculating the requisite majority, which is one half in value of the members unless the articles otherwise provide (r 1.20). The value of members' votes is determined by reference to the number of votes conferred on each member by the company's articles.[25]

As stated above, the proposal is deemed to have been rejected if the creditors' meeting and the members' meeting fail to approve it at or before the final adjourned meetings (r 1.21(6)).

(7) Report

Section 4(6) of IA 1986 requires the chairman to report the result of the meeting to the court within four days of the holding of the meeting (r 1.24(3)). The report must contain a statement on the fate of the proposals; set out each of the resolutions taken at the meeting and the decisions on each; list those present or represented at the meeting, the value of their votes and how they voted on the resolutions; and any other information of which the chairman thinks the court should be aware (r 1.24(2)). Where a voluntary arrangement has been approved, a copy of this report must also be sent to the Registrar (r 1.24(5)).

Notice of the results of the meeting should be sent to all persons who received notice of the meeting (r 1.24(4)).

(8) Challenge of decisions

A person entitled to vote at the meeting, the nominee or, if the company is being wound up or an administration order is in force, the liquidator or administrator may apply to revoke or suspend the approval of a voluntary arrangement on the grounds that it unfairly prejudices the interests of a creditor, member or contributory of the company or that there has been some material irregularity at or in relation to the meeting (s 6).[26] An application shall not be made after the end of the period of 28 days beginning with the first day on which each of the reports (mentioned above)

---

25   Insolvency (Amendment) Rules 1987, SI 1987/1919, r 3(1), Sch Pt 1, para 5.

26   For cases on what can constitute 'unfair prejudice' see the review of the cases concerning both individual and company voluntary arrangements in Stephen A Lawson *Individual Voluntary Arrangements*, 2nd edn (Jordans, 1996) at para 6.3.3, and see *March Estates plc v Gunmark Ltd* [1996] BPIR 439; *Lam Soon Australia Pty Ltd v Molit (No 55) Pty Ltd* [1997] BPIR 481; *Re Cardona* [1997] BPIR 604; and *Re Bielecki* [1998] BPIR 655. For cases on 'material irregularity' see ibid at para 6.3.4; *National Westminster Bank plc v Scher* [1998] BPIR 224, and *Duce v Commissioner of Inland Revenue* (unreported) 4 December 1998, ChD.

has been made to the court. The court has no power to extend the 28-day period.[27] In this context, it should be noted that unless express provision is made in the proposals as approved, the court has no jurisdiction to amend an arrangement without the unanimous consent of the creditors.[28] To assist creditors and the company in determining their rights to challenge the decision of the meeting, best practice requires that the responsible insolvency practitioner should always create a record of the meeting which should be prepared in accordance with SIP 12.

COMPANY ADMINISTRATION

(1) Creditors' meeting

Section 23(1)(b), IA 1986 requires an administrator to place a statement of his or her proposals for achieving the purposes specified in the administration order before a meeting of the company's creditors within three months of the making of the administration order. The creditors' meeting must be *held* and not merely summoned within the three-month period. The court has power to extend the three-month period.[29] Notwithstanding the desire of the legislature for speed, it must be accompanied by a useful gathering of intelligence to guide the company into the future. Speed for its own sake is something that should not be paramount.[30] The meeting is required to consider whether or not to approve the administrator's proposals (IA 1986, s 24(1)) and is entitled to approve the proposals with modifications providing the administrator consents to the modifications (IA 1986, s 24(2)). The administrator should include in his proposals full details of any connected party transaction undertaken or proposed in the period of two years prior to the making of the administration order and in the period since the making of that order.[31]

(2) Notice

Section 23(1)(b), IA 1986 provides for at least 14 days' notice of the meeting. Rule 2.18 requires notice to be given to all creditors and to all directors and officers who the administrator considers ought to be present at the meeting. A proxy form should accompany the notice (r 2.19(5)). Rules 8.1 to 8.7 deal with representation of a creditor by proxy. All proxies used must be retained by the chairman and

---

27 *Re Bournemouth & Boscombe Athletic Football Club Co Ltd* [1998] BPIR 183.
28 See *Re Alpa Lighting Ltd* [1997] BPIR 341.
29 See, eg, *Re Newport County Association Football Club Ltd* [1987] BCLC 582; *Re N S Distribution* [1990] BCLC 169; and *Cawthorne v Keira Construction Pty Ltd* (1994) 13 ACSR 337. For a case where no proposals could be formulated within the time allowed see *Re N S Distribution* [1990] BCLC 169.
30 *Re Tracker Software (Australia) Pty Ltd* (1997) 24 ACSR 92.
31 SIP 13, para 6.5

delivered to the responsible insolvency practitioner forthwith after the meeting who must, so long as they are in his hands, allow them to be inspected by the creditors at all reasonable times, on any business day (rr 8.4 and 8.5).[32] Notice of the meeting should also be advertised in the same newspaper in which the administration was advertised.

Unless the court otherwise directs, the meeting should be convened for a business day between the hours of 10.00 am and 4.00 pm (r 2.19(3)); and the venue should be fixed with respect to the convenience of the creditors (r 2.19(2)).

(3) Identity of creditors

The creditors required to be summoned to the meeting are all creditors identified in the statement of affairs and all other creditors known to the administrator who had outstanding claims against the company at the date of the administration order (r 2.18(1)). The identity of those creditors entitled to vote at the meeting is discussed below.

(4) Chairman[33]

The chairman at a meeting of this type must be the administrator or any person nominated by the administrator provided they are eligible to act as chairman. Eligible persons are either qualified insolvency practitioners in relation to the particular company, or employees of the administrator or the administrator's firm experienced in the handling of such matters (r 2.20).

As is the case with any company meeting, the chairman has considerable power with respect to the proceedings. In particular, with respect to creditors' meetings in an administration, the chairman may admit or reject the whole or part of a creditor's claim to vote (r 2.23(1)). If, however, the chairman is in any doubt about whether a creditor has a right to vote or not, then the chairman ought to mark the claim as objected to but nevertheless allow the creditor in question to vote (r 2.23(3)). Any challenge in court to the chairman's exercise of these powers must be made within 14 days from the delivery by the administrator of the report on the outcome of the meeting to the court, which is required under IA 1986, s 24(4). Given that the assets under administration are for the benefit of all creditors, the court will often be reluctant to interfere, but will allow issues to be resolved by the creditors in further meetings.[34]

It is the chairman's duty to see that minutes of the proceedings at the meeting are entered into the company's minute-book (r 2.28(2)). The minutes must include a

---

32 See generally Proxies on page 133 above.
33 For a recent review of the case-law relating to the powers and duties of a chairman of a meeting see *Link Agricultural Pty Ltd v Shanahan* (1998) 28 ACSR 498. See also *Re Chevron Furnishers Pty Ltd* (1992) 8 ACSR 726.
34 See, eg, *Re Ballan Pty Ltd* (1993–1994) 12 ACSR 605.

list of creditors who attended personally or by proxy and, if a creditors' committee has been established, the names and addresses of its members (r 2.28(3)).

(5) Adjournment

The Rules lay down three circumstances in which the meeting may be adjourned. First, the chairman may, and if a resolution is passed to that effect shall, adjourn the meeting if there is not the requisite majority approving the administrator's proposals. (The requisite majority is discussed below.) The meeting cannot be adjourned for more than 14 days on this ground (r 2.18(4)). Secondly, if there is no chairman within 30 minutes of the time set down for the commencement of the meeting then the meeting is adjourned to the same time and place in the following week. If the new time falls on a day which is not a business day (because, for example, it is a Bank Holiday), then the meeting is adjourned to the business day immediately following (r 2.19(6)). Thirdly, the chairman may exercise his or her discretion to adjourn the meeting for a period not exceeding 14 days (r 2.19(7)).

(6) Voting

The persons entitled to vote at a creditor's meeting of a company in administration are those creditors who have given the administrator details of the debt which is allegedly due from the company before noon on the business day before the meeting and which have had that debt approved (in accordance with r 2.22) and, where the creditor intends to vote by proxy, have lodged with the administrator the proxy intended to be used (r 2.22(1)). The chairman does, however, have a discretion to permit a person to vote even where they have failed to comply with these requirements (r 2.22(2)).[35]

Rule 2.22(1) requires that the details of the debt to be given to the administrator must include any calculation required under rr 2.24 to 2.27. As votes are calculated against the amounts of the creditor's debt (r 2.22(4)), these calculations are relevant to computing the voting power of each creditor. The calculations in rr 2.24 to 2.27 relate respectively to: secured creditors; holders of negotiable instruments; retention of title creditors; and hire purchase, conditional sale and chattel leasing agreements. In very general terms, they require creditors holding these types of interests to make an allowance in respect of the security which they hold. This allowance is deducted from the creditor's debt for the purpose of calculation of the creditor's vote.

The majority required is a simple one (r 2.28(1)), but a resolution will not be valid where more than half in value of the creditors vote against it provided that those creditors making up the half against the resolution are not, to the chairman's

---

35 For a case where the court allowed a trustee for bondholders to split its vote in respect of the debt owned to it to reflect the wishes of the bondholders see *Re Polly Peck International plc* [1991] BCC 503.

knowledge, persons connected with the company (r 2.28(1A)). Application of these rules may require a relatively time-consuming calculation, especially since creditors might be entitled to split their vote on the basis of value and vote a certain amount of value one way and a certain amount another.[36]

(7) Administrator's report

After the meeting the administrator must report the result of the meeting to the court (IA 1986, s 24(4)). Details of the proposals and any revisions or modifications to the proposals considered at the meeting should be annexed to the report (r 2.29). The report should also be sent to creditors (see r 2.30).

(8) Creditors' committee

The creditors' meeting may establish a creditors' committee (IA 1986, s 49). Rules 2.34 to 2.45 govern the meetings of such committees.

ADMINISTRATIVE RECEIVERSHIP

(1) Creditors' meeting

Within three months of the appointment of an administrative receiver, he or she must make a report in accordance with IA 1986, s 48(1) which must be sent to the Registrar, trustees for secured creditors, secured creditors and unsecured creditors. The obligation to send the report to the unsecured creditors can also be discharged by publishing a notice stating an address to which unsecured creditors may write in order to receive a copy of the report free of charge (IA 1986, s 48(2)). The administrative receiver is then required, unless the court otherwise directs, to lay a copy of the report before a meeting of the unsecured creditors (s 48(2)). The administrative receiver should include in his report full details regarding any connected party transactions (if any) prior to the meeting.[37] The court may only give a direction to the contrary if the administrative receiver's report states an intention to apply for such a direction and a copy of the report has been sent to all unsecured creditors (or a notice has been published inviting them to send for the report) at least 14 days before the hearing of the application for a direction. The only circumstance in which a meeting of unsecured creditors can be dispensed with without a direction from the court is where the company has gone into liquidation and the administrative receiver complies with the requirements of IA 1986, s 48(4).

---

36   *Re Polly Peck International plc* [1991] BCC 503.
37   SIP 13, para 6.5.

(2) Notice

At least 14 days' notice of the meeting must be given to all creditors identified in the statement of affairs and to any other creditors that the administrative receiver knows had a claim against the company at the date of his or her appointment (IA 1986, s 48(2); r 3.9(3)). The notice should also be published in the same newspaper in which the receiver's appointment was advertised (r 3.9(6)).

The notice must, of course, give the time and place of the meeting. The place of the meeting must be fixed having regard to the convenience of those entitled to attend (r 3.9(1)) and it must be held between 10.00 am and 4.00 pm on a business day (r 3.9(2)). In addition to stating time and place, the notice must also state: first, that creditors whose entire claim against the company is secured may not attend or be represented at the meeting (r 3.9(5)); and secondly, the effect of the provisions on voting rights in r 3.11(1) (r 3.9(11)). The notice must be accompanied by a proxy form (r 3.9(4)).

(3) Creditors entitled to participate in the meeting

As already noted, the meeting is a meeting of unsecured creditors. This means that secured creditors may only vote in respect of the balance of the debt due after deducting the value of the security held (r 3.11(6)). So far as creditors whose debt is secured by a bill of exchange or a promissory note are concerned, they may only vote if they are willing to treat the liability of every person liable antecedently to the company as security, or if they are prepared to estimate the value of the security and deduct it from their claim against the company for the purpose of calculating voting rights (r 3.11(7)).

No creditor qualified to vote may vote at the meeting unless they have given the administrative receiver details of the debt claimed to be due by 12 noon on the business day before the meeting and the claim has been admitted under r 3.11 (r 3.11(1)(a)). Where a creditor wishes to vote by proxy, the proxy must be lodged with the administrative receiver (r 3.11(1)(b)).

(4) Chairman[38]

The chairman at the meeting is the administrative receiver or a person nominated by the administrative receiver (r 3.10(1)). The administrative receiver may only nominate another person to be the chairman if that person is a qualified insolvency practitioner in relation to the company, or an employee of the receiver or the receiver's firm who is experienced in insolvency matters (r 3.10(2)).

---

38 For a recent review of the case-law relating to the powers and duties of a chairman of a meeting see *Link Agricultural Pty Ltd v Shanahan* (1998) 28 ACSR 498. See also *Re Chevron Furnishers Pty Ltd* (1992) 8 ACSR 726.

The Rules confer on the chairman a number of specific powers in addition to the chairman's usual powers to regulate the meeting. Most of the additional powers relate to qualification for voting. The chairman has, for instance, a discretion to allow a creditor who has failed to submit details in writing of the debt due from the company before 12 noon on the business day preceding the meeting to vote notwithstanding this omission (r 3.11(2)). The chairman may also call for the production of documents or evidence to support a creditor's claim (r 3.11(3)). The chairman may, whether he or she has called for the production of documents or other evidence or not, reject the whole or part of a creditor's entitlement to vote (r 3.12(1)); or, if unsure about the admissibility of a claim to be entitled to vote, mark it as objected to but allow it to proceed in the first instance (r 3.12(3)). The chairman's decision on entitlement to vote is subject to an appeal by any creditor to the court (r 3.12(2)) and if the chairman's decision is varied on appeal the court may summon another meeting or make any such order as it considers just (r 3.12(4); (see also r 3.12(5) as to costs of the appeal). Finally, the chairman is charged with the duty of ensuring that a record of the proceedings is made (r 3.15(2)). The record must show the names of the creditors attending in person or by proxy and, if a committee of creditors is appointed, the names and addresses of its members (r 3.15(3)).

(5) Adjournment

The power of adjournment resides solely in the chairman, who may adjourn the meeting to such time and place as he or she thinks fit (r 3.14(1)).

(6) Voting

As with the other types of creditors' meetings considered earlier, the vote is calculated by reference to the unsecured amount owing to the creditor (r 3.11(4)). Any amounts paid in respect of the debt since the appointment of the receiver should be deducted when making this calculation (r 3.11(4)). Since the size of the debt is relevant to making the calculation on voting power, a vote may not be cast in respect of an unliquidated or unascertained debt, unless the chairman agrees to an estimated minimum value for the purpose of calculating the voting power of a creditor holding such a debt (r 3.11(5)). This power to estimate a minimum value is also subject to appeal to the court under r 3.12(2), see above.

The required majority for passing a resolution at this type of creditors' meeting is a simple majority in value of those voting (r 3.15(1)).

(7) Creditors' committee

One of the things which the creditors' meeting in an administrative receivership may do is to establish a creditors' committee to assist the administrative receiver in the discharge of his or her functions (IA 1986, s 49 and r 3.18(1)). The proceedings at meetings of such a committee are governed by rr 3.18 to 3.30A.

MEMBERS' VOLUNTARY WINDING UP

A voluntary winding up may be either a members' voluntary winding up or a creditors' voluntary winding up. It will be a members' voluntary winding up where the directors have made a statutory declaration of solvency in accordance with IA 1986, s 89 (IA 1986, s 90).

A number of company meetings are required in order to effect a members' voluntary winding up. First, there must be a meeting in which it is resolved to wind the company up. This meeting must pass an ordinary resolution that the company be wound up where the duration of the company as fixed by the articles expires or an event occurs on the occurrence of which the articles provide that the company is to be dissolved (IA 1986, s 84(1)(a)); a special resolution that the company be wound up voluntarily (s 84(1)(b)) or an extraordinary resolution to the effect that winding up is advisable due to the fact that the company's liabilities prevent it continuing its business (s 84(1)(c)). Secondly, the company must hold a meeting to appoint liquidators (IA 1986, s 91(1)) and, if necessary, to fill any vacancy in the position of liquidator (IA 1986, s 92(1)). Thirdly, if the winding-up process lasts for more than a year the liquidator must summon a general meeting of the company at the end of the first year from the commencement of the winding up and each succeeding year (IA 1986, s 93(1)) so that the liquidator can lay before the meeting an account of his or her handling of the winding up (IA 1986, s 93(2)). Finally, once the company's affairs are fully wound up the liquidator must call a final meeting and lay before it an account of the winding up of the company's affairs (IA 1986, s 94(1)).

Subject to the qualifications noted here, these meetings are held in accordance with the usual procedures and conduct for company meetings. So far as the initial meeting is concerned, an additional obligation is the requirement that notice of the resolution be given in the *Gazette* within 14 days of its passing (IA 1986, s 85); also, in order for the winding up to be a members' voluntary winding up, the directors' statutory declaration of solvency must be made within the five weeks immediately preceding the passing of the resolution (IA 1986, s 89(2)(a)).

No special requirements are made in respect of the meeting to appoint the liquidator, although it should be noted that once appointed the liquidator comes under an obligation to publicise and give notice to certain parties of his or her appointment (see r 4.106). This also applies to any liquidator appointed to fill a casual vacancy. Where a meeting has to be held to fill such a casual vacancy, this must be convened by a contributory (the concept of 'contributory' is discussed below) or by any continuing liquidators (IA 1986, s 92(2)). The reason for this is that at the time of the initial appointment of a liquidator the directors' powers generally cease (IA 1986, s 91(2)). Aside from the special arrangements for convening a meeting to fill a casual vacancy in the office of liquidator, such a meeting is held in the usual manner unless otherwise determined by the court (IA 1986, s 92(3)).

As has already been noted, any general meetings called where the winding up lasts for more than one year, and also the final meeting prior to dissolution, must be convened by the liquidator. Again, this is a consequence of the cessation of the directors' powers. Certain other deviations from the normal procedure are also prescribed in respect of the final meeting prior to dissolution. First, the meeting is to be called by an advertisement in the *Gazette*, published at least a month before the meeting, specifying its time, place and object (IA 1986, s 94(2)). Secondly, within a week of holding the meeting, the liquidator must make a return to the Registrar specifying that the meeting is taking place on a certain date and must send the Registrar a copy of the account laid before the final meeting (IA 1986, s 94(3) and see the Insolvency Rules, Form 4.71 as to the form of the return). If the final meeting is inquorate then the liquidator's return should note that the meeting was duly summoned but was inquorate (IA 1986, s 94(5)). The filing of the final account and return with the Registrar starts the process of dissolution of the company which, in the ordinary case, is deemed to have occurred within three months of the filing (IA 1986, s 201(2), but note the power of the court in s 201(3) and (4) to defer the date of dissolution).

CREDITORS' VOLUNTARY WINDING UP[39]

(1) Meetings to be held

As already noted, a voluntary winding up will be a creditors' voluntary winding up where the directors have not made a declaration of solvency in accordance with IA 1986, s 89 (IA 1986, s 90). There is also provision for a members' voluntary winding up to be converted to a creditors' voluntary winding up (IA 1986, s 96).

The same types of meetings are required in a creditors' voluntary winding up as for a members' voluntary winding up with the added complication that separate creditors' meetings are required for all the types of meetings listed in relation to members' voluntary winding up except the initial meeting of the company at which the resolution to wind up is passed. In a creditors' voluntary winding up, once the initial resolution has been passed by the company, the next meeting required is a meeting of creditors (IA 1986, s 98) at which the directors must lay a statement of

---

39 Specific guidance to insolvency practitioners on summoning and holding meetings of creditors convened pursuant to s 98 of the Insolvency Act 1986 can be found in SIP 8 which provides a thorough overview of the conduct of such meetings.

affairs before the creditors in accordance with IA 1986, s 99. This first meeting of creditors may also appoint a liquidator (IA 1986, s 100; see s 100(3) with respect to the situation where the creditors' and the members' meeting nominate different liquidators) and a liquidation committee (IA 1986, s 101). (See, further, r 4.53 as to the business of the first meeting of creditors.) The creditors may also fill any casual vacancy in the office of liquidator (IA 1986, s 104). If the winding up has been converted from a members' voluntary winding up to a creditors' voluntary winding up then the first creditors' meeting does not need to be held as its function will already have been satisfied by the creditors' meeting held in accordance with IA 1986, s 95, which is necessary for the conversion to a creditors' voluntary winding up (IA 1986, s 96). The other meetings which must be held in a creditors' voluntary winding up are creditors' and members' meetings held annually where the winding up lasts more than a year, and final creditors' and members' meetings prior to dissolution. The liquidator may also, at any time, summon meetings of creditors and contributories in order to ascertain their wishes (see r 4.54). Similarly, creditors may requisition meetings (see r 4.57). The procedure for the holding of all the members' meetings in a creditors' voluntary winding up is the same as that discussed above in relation to a members' voluntary winding up. The creditors' meetings are, however, subject to special provisions in both the Insolvency Act 1986 and the Insolvency Rules. SIP 12 requires that the responsible insolvency practitioner should always create a record of the meeting which should be prepared in accordance with the provisions set out in SIP 12.

(2) Section 98 meeting

The first meeting of creditors under IA 1986, s 98 must be summoned by the company within 14 days from the day upon which the resolution for winding up is to be proposed (IA 1986, s 98(1)(a)). Unless the court makes an order under r 4.59 that the notice of the meeting is to be given by public advertisement rather than individually, the notice must be sent to the creditors by post at least seven days before the day on which the meeting is to be held (IA 1986, s 98(1)(b)) and the notice must be advertised in the *Gazette* and in at least two newspapers circulating in the locality of the company's principal place of business (IA 1986, s 98(1)(c); see IA 1986, s 98(3) and (4) where the company has more than one principal place of business or the principal place of business is not in the UK). Past and present officers may also be summoned to attend the meeting in accordance with r 4.58.

The notice must specify the time and place of the meeting and the place where proxies are to be lodged (r 4.51(2)). Reading together r 4.51(2) and r 4.60(2), it appears that the first meeting of creditors must be held between 12 noon and 4.00 pm on a business day. The venue must be fixed with regard to the convenience of the creditors (r 4.60(1)). The notice must also state one of the following: the name of a qualified insolvency practitioner who will furnish the creditors free of charge with any information they reasonably require about the company's affairs;[40] or an address at which, during the two days preceding the date for the meeting, a list of the names and addresses of the company creditors will be available free of charge (IA 1986, s 98(2)). The notice must be accompanied by a proxy form (r 4.60(3)).

A summary or a copy of the directors' sworn statement of affairs should be handed to all those attending the meeting, including a list of the names of the major creditors and the amounts owing to them. Guidance as to the information to be given to the meeting is set out in SIP 8 (para 36) and should include:

(i)   details of any prior involvement of the insolvency practitioner with the company or its directors;
(ii)   a detailed report of the previously held shareholders' meeting;
(iii) details of the costs paid or payable by the company for the statement of affairs and the convening of the meeting and any insolvency advice received;
(iv)   a detailed account of the company's relevant trading history; and
(v)   details of transactions with connected persons during the period of one year prior to the resolution of the directors that the company should be wound up.[41]

(3) Subsequent meetings: notice

Annual meetings of creditors must be summoned by the liquidator within three months of the end of the year in question (IA 1986, s 105(1)). Twenty-one days' notice specifying the purpose of the meeting (r 4.54(3)) must be given to all creditors known to the liquidator or identified in the company's statement of affairs (r 4.54(2)(a)), although the court may order the notice of meetings to be by public advertisement only (r 4.59). The liquidator may also summon company personnel (r 4.58(2)). The place of the meeting must be fixed having regard to the convenience of the creditors (r 4.60(1)) and it must be held between 10.00 am and 4.00 pm on a business day (r 4.60(2)). In addition to stating these matters, the notice must also state a time and place not more than four days before the meeting for the lodging of proxies (r 4.54(5)). A proxy form must accompany the notice (r 4.60(3)). No proxy form shall be pre-completed by the insertion in it of the name or description of any person (ie for appointment as an insolvency office holder or for appointment as a member of a committee or as proxy holder) (r 8.2).[42] Rules 8.1

---

40   This will normally include information included in the statement of affairs and the list of creditors, when available.
41   This is recognised as such an important area of potential concern to creditors attending the meeting that it is subject to separate practice guidance (SIP 13) entitled 'Acquisition of assets of insolvent companies by directors' (see in particular paras 4.2 and 5 which deal with recommended advice and disclosure which the insolvency practitioner should give to the directors and creditors respectively).
42   See SIP 10.

to 8.7 deal generally with representation of a creditor by proxy. There is a requirement for proxies to be signed by the principal or by a person authorised by him, in which case the nature of the authority must be stated. Proxies which are unsigned or which do not explain the authority under which they are signed will be invalid.[43]

At least 28 days' notice of the final meeting before dissolution must be given to all creditors who have proved their debts (r 4.126(1)). An advertisement stating the time, place and object of the meeting must also be published in the *Gazette* at least one month before the meeting (IA 1986, s 106(2)). Otherwise the rules on notice for this meeting are the same as for the annual creditors' meetings.

(4) Creditors' meetings: chairman[44]

Where the directors of a company nominate one of their number pursuant to s 99(1)(c) to preside at the s 98 meeting and that person fails to attend, those who do attend may appoint their own nominee as chairman.[45]

Except at the first meetings of creditors, the chairman at meetings of creditors in a creditors' voluntary winding up should be the liquidator or a person nominated by the liquidator (r 4.56). A person nominated by the liquidator must be a qualified insolvency practitioner in relation to the company, or an employee of the liquidator or the liquidator's firm with experience in insolvency matters (r 4.56(2)). At the first meeting of creditors, the chairman must be a director appointed by the other directors for that purpose (IA 1986, s 99(1)).

The Rules confer specific powers and duties on the chairman of a creditors' meeting. The chairman has a discretion in relation to the admission to the meeting of company personnel (r 4.58(5)); certain discretions in relation to adjournment, which are discussed below; a discretion in relation to admitting the votes of creditors who have failed to satisfy the rules on lodging proofs where the chairman believes that the failure was beyond the creditor's control (r 4.68); discretion to admit or reject any creditors' proof with respect to entitlement to vote (r 4.70(1)) or to mark a proof as objected to in the usual way (r 4.70(3)). The chairman's decisions on entitlement to vote may be appealed to the court by any creditor or contributory (r 4.70(2)). On such an appeal, the court is not limited to consideration of the evidence which was before the chairman but comes to a conclusion on

---

43   See generally Proxies on page 133 above.

44   For a recent review of the case-law relating to the powers and duties of a chairman of a meeting see *Link Agricultural Pty Ltd v Shanahan* (1998) 28 ACSR 498. See also *Re Chevron Furnishers Pty Ltd* (1992) 8 ACSR 726.

45   *Re Salcombe Hotel Development Corporation Ltd* [1991] BCLC 44.

all the evidence subsequently filed at court whether on balance a creditor's proof should be admitted in whole or in part for voting purposes.[46]

Where the chairman holds a proxy instructing the chairman to vote for a particular resolution and that resolution is not proposed by anyone else, then the chairman is required to propose it unless there is a good reason, in the chairman's view, for not doing so (r 4.64(a)). If the chairman does not propose a resolution in these circumstances, he or she must notify the appointor of the proxy of the reason for this immediately after the meeting (r 4.64(b)).

The other specific duties imposed on the chairman are keeping minutes as part of the record of the liquidation (r 4.71(1)), and keeping a list of all creditors attending the meeting (r 4.71(2)). This list should be made available for inspection to anyone attending the meeting.

Nominations for the appointment of a liquidator should be requested before any vote is taken. The holder of a proxy requiring him to vote for a particular liquidator is required to nominate that person, and it is therefore possible that the chairman or any other holder of such proxies may need to make more than one nomination.[47] It is acceptable in the first instance for a vote to be taken on an informal show of hands and if the result is accepted by all interested parties, the chairman may conclude that a resolution has been passed. If a formal vote becomes necessary, it should be conducted by stating the names of all those nominated and by the issue of voting papers on which those wishing to vote will be required to show their name, the name of the creditor they are representing, the amount of the creditor's claim and the name of the nominated person for whom they wish to vote. When all votes have been counted, the chairman should announce the result to the meeting, giving details of the total value of votes cast in favour of each nomination. He should also give details of votes which have been rejected, either in whole or in part, and should also state which nomination those creditors supported and the reasons for the rejection. An absolute majority is required and if the first poll is not conclusive, the nominee receiving the least votes will be excluded from the next (and each successive) poll where no other nominee has withdrawn.[48]

(5) Creditors' meetings: adjournment and suspension

The chairman of a creditors' meeting has power not only to adjourn the meeting in his or her discretion (r 4.65(3) and (4)), but also, during the course of the meeting, to suspend it once for up to one hour (r 4.65(2)). The chairman must adjourn the meeting if the meeting so resolves (r 4.65(3)). The adjourned meeting will be held at such time or place as the chairman determines (r 4.65(3) and (4)). However, this discretion is qualified to the extent that the adjournment may not be for more than

---

46   *Re A Company (No 004539 of 1993)* [1995] BCC 116 at 120(F–G).
47   SIP 8, para 43.
48   SIP 8, paras 45–7. As to the appointment of a creditors' committee, see ibid, para 48.

21 days and the usual rules (r 4.60(1) and (2)) as to fixing the time and place of meetings apply (r 4.65(5)). The meeting will also be adjourned where there is no chairman present and none is agreed upon (r 4.65(6)). In this case, the adjournment will be to the same time and place in the following week, unless that falls on a day which is not a business day, in which case the meeting will be adjourned to the next business day following that day (r 4.65(6)). Where the meeting has been adjourned, proofs and proxies may be lodged any time before midday on the business day before the adjourned meeting (r 4.65(7)). Except where the meeting has been adjourned because there is no chairman, the chairman should give notice of adjournments to any of the company's personnel, not present at the meeting, as he or she thinks appropriate (r 4.58(3)).

Finally, it should be noted that a special provision is made with respect to the circumstances where the meeting of the company at which the resolution to wind up is to be proposed under IA 1986, s 84 is adjourned and the first meeting of creditors takes place before it. Where this happens then any resolution passed at the first meeting of creditors will not take effect until the company passes a resolution to wind up (r 4.53A).

(6) Creditors' meeting: voting

A person is only entitled to vote at a creditors' meeting in a creditors' voluntary winding up if they have lodged a proof of debt and the claim to vote has been admitted by the chairman under r 4.70(1) (r 4.67(1)(a)). If a creditor wishes to vote by proxy they must also lodge the proxy as required in the notice for the meeting (r 4.67(1)(b)). The chairman's power to allow a creditor to vote without proving their debt (r 4.68) has been noted above. The court also has the power in exceptional circumstances to allow creditors, or a class of creditors, to vote without proving their debts (r 4.67(2)).

As in other types of creditors' meetings considered in this chapter, voting power is calculated by reference to the value of the debt owed (r 4.63(1)). Similarly, for the purpose of calculating voting rights, deductions must be made in respect of any type of security (r 4.67(4) and (5)(b)) or the holders of bills of exchange and promissory notes must treat the liability of those antecedent to the company as security (r 4.67(5)(a)), and an estimated minimum amount must be placed upon unliquidated or unascertained debts (r 4.67(3)).

The required majority is a simple majority in value of those voting (r 4.63(1)), although on any resolution affecting the office of liquidator the vote of the liquidator or any partner or employee of the liquidator cannot be counted as part of the majority (r 4.63(4)).

(7) Return to Registrar on final meetings prior to dissolution

In a creditors' voluntary winding up the liquidator must send a copy of the account of the liquidation which has been laid before the final members' meeting and the final creditors' meeting and a return concerning both meetings to the Registrar (see Insolvency Rules, Form 4.72) in the same way as required in respect of the final members' meeting in a members' voluntary winding up, as discussed above (IA 1986, s 106). As in a members' voluntary winding up, this triggers the dissolution of the company which will occur within three months of the filing (IA 1986, s 201(2)), subject to the court's power to defer the date of dissolution (s 201(3) and (4)).

WINDING UP BY THE COURT

(1) Meetings to be held

The circumstances in which a company may be wound up by the court are contained in IA 1986, s 122. One of those circumstances is that the company has resolved by special resolution to that effect (s 122(1)(a)). Where this is relevant, the special resolution should be passed in the same manner as any other special resolution of the company. Six other possible circumstances leading to a winding up by the court are also listed; thus, in many cases it is not unlikely that there will be no initial meeting of the company to pass a special resolution for winding up by the court.

Once winding up by the court has commenced, the official receiver must decide within 12 weeks, beginning on the day the winding-up order was made, whether or not to exercise the power under IA 1986, s 136(4) to summon separate meetings of creditors and contributories for the purpose of choosing someone other than the official receiver to be the liquidator (s 136(5)(a)). The official receiver is required to exercise the power to call such meetings when requested to by one-quarter in value of the company's creditors. The choice of the liquidator at such meetings of creditors and contributories is governed by IA 1986, s 139. Such meetings may also appoint a liquidation committee (IA 1986, s 141; see, further, r 4.52 as to the business of such meetings). Meetings summoned by the official receiver under the power in IA 1986, s 136(4) are referred to in the Rules (and in this part of this chapter), respectively, as 'the first meeting of creditors' and 'the first meeting of contributories' and together as 'the first meetings in liquidation' (r 4.50(7)).

Where the liquidator is not the official receiver, a final meeting of creditors must be summoned by the liquidator at which the liquidator's report on the winding up should be presented and the meeting should determine whether to release the liquidator (IA 1986, s 146(1)). As in a creditors' voluntary winding up, the official receiver or the liquidator also has the power to call meetings of creditors or of contributories in order to ascertain their wishes (r 4.54); and the creditors or contributories may also requisition a meeting (r 4.57). As will be seen, these are only some of a number of similarities in the rules on meetings of creditors in a creditors' voluntary winding up and meetings of creditors or contributories in a winding up by the court. The discussion below seeks to highlight the differences rather than repeating provisions in the Rules common to both types of winding up.

(2) Contributories

A contributory is any person liable to contribute to the company in the event of its winding up (IA 1986, s 79).

(3) Notice

Where the official receiver decides to exercise the power to call first meetings of creditors and contributories, he or she must fix venues for each meeting within four months of the winding-up order (r 4.50(1)). Where the official receiver is required by the creditors to call first meetings under IA 1986, s 136(5)(c), he or she must fix a venue within three months of the receipt of the request (r 4.50(6)(b)). At least 21 days' notice of each meeting must be given to the court and, respectively, to every creditor known to the official receiver or identified in the statement of affairs, and to every person appearing in the company's books or otherwise as a contributory (r 4.50(2)). The notices must specify the usual matters regarding time and place, as discussed above (r 4.60(1) and (2)) and must be accompanied by a proxy form (r 4.60(3)). Additionally, the notice must specify a time not more than four days before the meeting for the lodgement of, in the case of a creditors' meeting, proofs and proxies and, in the case of a contributories' meeting, proxies (r 4.50(4)). Notice of the meetings must also be publicly advertised (r 4.50(5)).

For the final meeting of creditors at least 28 days' notice must be given to all creditors who have proved their debts and the notice should also appear in the *Gazette* at least one month before the meeting (r 4.125(1); and see Insolvency Rules, Form 4.22).

(4) Chairman[49]

Where a meeting in a winding up by the court is convened by the official receiver, as will be the case for the first meetings in liquidation, then the official receiver or a person nominated in writing by the official receiver is the chairman (r 4.55(2)). A written nomination is not necessary, however, where the person nominated is another official receiver or a deputy official receiver. Where the convenor is not the official receiver, as will be the case for the final meeting summoned by the

---

49 For a recent review of the case-law relating to the powers and duties of a chairman of a meeting see *Link Agricultural Pty Ltd v Shanahan* (1998) 28 ACSR 498. See also *Re Chevron Furnishers Pty Ltd* (1992) 8 ACSR 726.

liquidator under IA 1986, s 146, then the convenor or a person nominated in writing by the convenor is the chairman (r 4.55(3)). However, where the convenor is not the official receiver, the convenor may only nominate another person as chairman if that person is a qualified insolvency practitioner in relation to the company or an employee of the liquidator or the liquidator's firm experienced in insolvency matters (r 4.55(3)).

The powers and duties of the chairman in creditors' and contributories' meetings in a winding up by the court are the same as those in a creditors' voluntary winding up (as discussed above), except for the following two matters. First, in a winding up by the court the chairman does not have a discretion to allow a creditor to vote notwithstanding the creditor's failure to comply with the rules on lodging proofs of debt by a certain tune, although the chairman still has the same power to admit or reject a proof for the purpose of entitlement to vote (r 4.70(1)). Secondly, in a winding up by the court the chairman must not only make a record of resolutions passed (r 4.71(3)), he or she must also file certified particulars of such resolutions in court within 21 days of the meeting (r 4.71(4)).

(5) Adjournment

The rules on adjournment are the same for creditors' and contributories' meetings in a winding up by the court as they are for creditors' meetings in a creditors' voluntary winding up.

(6) Voting

Subject to the absence of the chairman's discretion to allow a creditor to vote where the creditor has failed to lodge a proof by the due date (as discussed above), the rules on voting are the same for creditors' and contributories' meetings in a winding up by the court as they are for creditors' meetings in a creditors' voluntary winding up.

(7) Report to the court

After the final meeting of creditors required under IA 1986, s 146 has been held, the liquidator must give notice to the court of the holding of the meeting (see Insolvency Rules, Form 4.42) and a copy of the report must be sent to the official receiver. The notice must state whether or not the meeting has resolved to release the liquidator and must be accompanied by a copy of the report laid before the final meeting by the liquidator (r 4.125(4)). This report must give an account of the winding up including, in particular, a summary of receipts and payments and a statement by the liquidator that the account given has been reconciled with that held by the Secretary of State with respect to the winding up (r 4.125(2)). If the final meeting is inquorate, the liquidator must report this fact to the court, in which case the meeting is deemed to have been held and the liquidator deemed released (r 4.125(5)).

Appendix

PRECEDENTS FOR COMPANY MEETINGS[1]

CONTENTS

---

1   These precedents are based on selected precedents from *Jordans Company Secretarial Precedents* 2nd edn (Jordans, 1997).

2   The following devices are employed throughout these precedents:

    – [*italic text*] gives instructions on what details are to be inserted;

    – [roman text] gives examples or options of details to be inserted;

    – (round brackets) gives text to be deleted as applicable.

Precedent 1

Notice of Board Meeting

Notice is hereby given that a meeting of the directors of the company will be held at [*address*] at [*time*] [*date*] at which your attendance is requested.

_____   [*date*]

Secretary

Precedent 2

Specimen Agenda for Board Meeting

AGENDA

1. Apologies for absence.
2. Declaration of matters in which directors have an interest under Section 317 of the Companies Act 1985.
3. Minutes of meeting held on [*date*].
4. Matters arising therefrom.
5. Management accounts for [the three months ended 30 June *year*].
6. Divisional reports.
7. Audit review.
8. Employment policy.
9. Share transfers.
10. Other business.

Precedent 3

Annual General Meeting

(a) Notice and Agenda

Company number: [   ]

NOTICE OF ANNUAL GENERAL MEETING
OF [   ] LIMITED

THIS IS NOTICE THAT the Annual General Meeting of the above-named Company will be held at [*place*] on [*date*] at [*time*] for the following purposes.

1.   To receive the report of the directors and audited accounts, together with the audited report thereon, for the year ended [   ] 19[   ].
2.   To re-elect newly appointed directors.
3.   To re-elect the auditors.
4.   To authorise the directors to fix the remuneration of the auditors.

The date of this notice is: [*date*]

_____

Company Secretary

The registered office of the Company is: [*registered office address*]

NOTE: A Member of the Company who is entitled to attend and vote at the above-mentioned meeting is entitled to appoint a proxy,[1] who need not be a Member of the Company, to attend and vote instead of him.

Copies of service contracts of the directors with the company and any subsidiaries not expiring or determinable without payment of compensation within one year will be available during normal business hours, from the date of this notice until the conclusion of the meeting.

(b) Specimen Minutes of AGM

Minutes of the [10th] AGM held at [*place*] **on** [*date*].

PRESENT: _____ (Chairman)

_____ (Director)

_____ (Director)

_____ (Director)

(and the members who signed the attendance sheet attached to these minutes).

IN ATTENDANCE:[2]

_____ (Secretary)
_____ (Auditors)

(and   _____
        _____)

1. The secretary read the notice of meeting.

2. The chairman proposed:

    'That the report of the directors and the audited accounts for the year
    [19   ] now submitted to this meeting, be and are hereby
    received; and

    (That the final dividend of [   ]p per share recommended therein be
    and is hereby declared payable on [*date*] 19[   ] to holders of ordinary
    shares registered at the close of business on [*date*] 19[   ])'.

    [*Name*] seconded the resolution, which was put to the meeting and declared
    carried.

3. The chairman proposed:

    'That _____
    the director(s) retiring by rotation be and [is *or* are] hereby re-elected [a]
    director(s) of the company'.[3]

    [*Name*] seconded the resolution, which was put to the meeting and declared
    carried.

4. The chairman proposed:

    'That the appointment(s) of [*names*] to the Board on [*dates*] be
    confirmed'.

    [*Name*] seconded the resolution, which was put to the meeting and declared
    carried.

5. The chairman proposed:

'That Messrs [*name*] be re-appointed as auditors of the company, to hold office until the conclusion of the next general meeting at which accounts are laid and the directors be authorised to fix their remuneration'.

[*Name*] seconded the resolution which was put to the meeting and declared carried.

6.   There being no further business the meeting was closed.

_____

Chairman

_____

Notes

1 For a form of proxy, see Precedent 9.
2 Persons who are 'in attendance' at a meeting (rather than being 'present') are those who are not constituents of the meeting, ie in this case, not members or directors.
3 Under Table A, any director appointed by the directors since the previous AGM retires at the AGM, but may stand for re-election.

Precedent 4

Form of Notice of EGM to consider Particular Resolution

THIS IS NOTICE THAT an Extraordinary General Meeting of the Members of the above-named Company will be held at [*place*] on [*date*] at [*time*].

The business of the meeting will be to consider and, if thought fit, to pass the following resolutions which will be proposed as [ordinary *or* special] resolutions:

SPECIAL RESOLUTIONS

[*text of resolutions*]

The date of this notice is: [*date*]

By order of the Board

_____

Company Secretary

The registered office of the company is:

[*registered office address*]

A Member of the Company who is entitled to attend and vote at the above-mentioned meeting is entitled to appoint a proxy,[1] who need not be a Member of the Company, to attend and vote instead of him.

_____

Note

1 For a form of proxy, see Precedent 9.

Precedent 5

Special Notice to Propose Resolution

The Directors

[*company name*]   Limited

I hereby give special notice, pursuant to sections 379 and 388 of the Companies Act 1985, of my intention to propose the following resolution as an ordinary resolution at an extraordinary general meeting of the company: [*resolution*]

[*Date*]

Note

1 The following words should be included against the resolution in the notice of meeting:

'Special Notice has been received of the intention to propose this resolution'.

Precedent 6

Forms of Consent to the Holding of an EGM at Short Notice

Company number: [   ]
Company limited by shares
  [*company name*]   Limited

[Ordinary Resolution(s)

We, the undersigned, being the holders of not less than 95% in nominal value of the issued voting shares of the above-named Company, hereby consent to the holding of an Extraordinary General Meeting of the Company at the time and place and for the purpose set out in the notice convening the meeting which is attached to this form (notwithstanding that the meeting is called by shorter notice than that specified in section 369 of the Companies Act 1985).

or

[Special Resolution(s)

We, the undersigned, being the holders of not less than 95% in nominal value of the issued voting shares of the above-named Company, hereby consent to the holding of an Extraordinary General Meeting of the Company at the time and place and for the purposes set out in the notice convening the meeting which is attached to this form (notwithstanding that the meeting is called by shorter notice than that specified in section 378(2) of the Companies Act 1985).

Ordinary Resolution(s) and Special Resolution(s)

We, the undersigned, being the holders of not less than 95% in nominal value of the issued voting shares of the above-named Company, hereby consent to the holding of an Extraordinary General Meeting of the Company at the time and place and for the purpose set out in the notice convening the meeting which is attached to this form (notwithstanding that the meeting is called by shorter notice than that specified in sections 369 and 378(2) of the Companies Act 1985).]

Dated [*date*]   [*year*].

Name: _____   Signed: _____

Name: _____   Signed: _____

Name: _____   Signed: _____

Name: _____   Signed: _____

Name: _____   Signed: _____

Precedent 7

Consent to Short Notice for AGM

To the Directors of [*company name*] Limited

We, the undersigned, being all the members entitled to attend and vote at general meetings of the above-named company, do hereby signify our consent to the annual general meeting of the company being held on [*date*] notwithstanding that the meeting is called by shorter notice than that specified in section 369 of the Companies Act 1985 [and do hereby agree that copies of the documents required to be sent in accordance with section 238(1) of the Companies Act 1985 shall be deemed to have been duly sent notwithstanding that they are sent less than 21 days before the date of the said meeting].

Dated [*date*] [*year*].

_____

_____

_____

[*signatures of all members*]

Precedent 8

Form of Written Resolution in lieu of Meeting

Company No [   ]

THE COMPANIES ACTS 1985 TO 1989

PRIVATE COMPANY LIMITED BY SHARES

WRITTEN RESOLUTION(S) OF [*company name*] LIMITED

Dated this [*day*] day of [*month*] [*year*].

We, the undersigned, being all the members[1] of the company who, at the date of this resolution would be entitled to attend and vote at general meetings of the company, HEREBY PASS the following resolutions as [a] [special *or* extraordinary *or* ordinary *or* elective] resolution(s)[2] and agree that the said resolution(s) shall, for all purposes be as valid and effective as if the same had been passed by us all at a general meeting of the company duly convened and held.

Notes

1 If a class resolution is sent, detail here, eg 'of the class of seven per cent cumulative preference shares in the capital of the'.

[2] If the resolution is passed under the provisions of Table A, as opposed to the statutory procedures introduced under s 113 of the Companies Act 1989, the following paragraph should be added to the written resolution:

'We confirm that this written resolution is passed in accordance with regulation 53 of Table A to the Companies Act 1985, which is embodied in the articles of association of the company.'

Precedent 9

Form of Proxy
(SPECIAL OR GENERAL POWER)

pursuant to section 372(a) of the Companies Act 1985
and Table A, reg 61

J372a

.... Limited.

I ....

of ....

in the County of .... being a Member of

.... LIMITED,

hereby appoint ....

of ....

or failing him ....

of ....

as my Proxy, to vote for me on my behalf at the* ....

GENERAL MEETING of the Company to be held on the ....

day of .... 19 ...., and at any adjournment thereof.

This form is to be used in respect of the resolutions mentioned below
as follows:

Resolution No 1   †for †against
Resolution No 2   †for †against

[*dated*]

.... *Signature*
of Member

N.B. – This form must be deposited at the Registered Office of the Company at ....
.... not less than [forty eight] .... hours before the time for holding the meeting.
* "Annual" or "Extraordinary" as the case may be.   † Strike out whichever is not desired.
Unless otherwise instructed, the proxy will vote as he thinks fit.

Precedent 10

Elective Resolution

(a) Election to Dispense with AGM

ELECTIVE RESOLUTION

That pursuant to section 366A of the Companies Act 1985, the company hereby elects to dispense with the holding of annual general meetings in [*year*] and subsequent years.[1]

(b) Election to Dispense with Laying of Accounts and Reports Before General Meeting

ELECTIVE RESOLUTION

That pursuant to section 252 of the Companies Act 1985, the company hereby elects to dispense with the laying of accounts and reports before the company in general meeting.[2]

(c) Election to Dispense with Annual Appointment of Auditors

ELECTIVE RESOLUTION

That pursuant to section 386 of the Companies Act 1985 the company hereby elects to dispense with the obligation to appoint auditors annually.

Notes

1 This election has effect in the year in which it is made and subsequent years, but does not effect any liability already incurred by reason of default in holding an AGM.

2 This election has effect in relation to the accounts and reports in respect of the financial year in which it is passed, and subsequently financial years, but *not* previous financial years.

Precedent 11

Members' Requisition for EGM

[*Date*]

To [*company name*] Limited and its Directors

We, the undersigned, being shareholders who, at the date of deposit of this requisition at the registered office of the company, hold not less than one-tenth of the paid up capital of the company, hereby requisition an extraordinary general meeting of the company in accordance with section 368 of the Companies Act 1985 to consider and, if thought fit, to pass the resolutions set out below as special resolutions.

The resolutions to be proposed are as follows.

1.   [That the articles of association of the company be amended by the deletion of subclause (c) of Article 7 from the said articles.]
2.   That the company meet the costs of convening and holding this meeting and circulating the statement of the requisitionists with respect to the resolutions to be proposed.

Should Resolution No 2 not be passed, we undertake to meet the costs of the company in giving effect to this requisition.

Yours faithfully

_____

_____

[*Signatures*]

Precedent 12

Enhanced Voting Rights for Directors

1. Every director for the time being of the Company shall have the following rights:

    (a) if at any general meeting a poll is duly demanded on a resolution to remove him from office, to ten votes for each share of which he is the holder; and

    (b) if at any general meeting a poll is duly demanded on a resolution having the effect of deleting, amending or nullifying the effect of the provisions of this Article, to ten votes for each share of which he is the holder if voting against such resolution.

2. Regulation 54 in Table A shall be modified accordingly.

Precedent 13

Article for use where Directors' Meetings are to be held Electronically

MEETINGS

1. In this Article 'electronic' means actuated by electric, magnetic, electro-magnetic, electro-chemical or electro-mechanical energy and 'by electronic means' means by any manner only capable of being so actuated.
2. A person in communication by electronic means with the chairman and with all other parties to a meeting of the directors or of a committee of the directors shall be regarded for all purposes as personally attending such a meeting provided that but only for so long as at such a meeting he has the ability to communicate interactively and simultaneously with all other parties attending the meeting including all persons attending by electronic means.
3. A meeting at which one or more of the directors attends by electronic means is deemed to be held at such place as the directors shall at the said meeting resolve. In the absence of a resolution as aforesaid, the meeting shall be deemed to be held at the place, if any, where a majority of the directors attending the meeting are physically present, or in default of such a majority, the place at which the chairman of the meeting is physically present.

INDEX

Page references set in **bold** are to precedents